WATERS DARK AND DEEP

One New Orleans Family's Rescue
Amid the Devastation of Hurricane Katrina

OCT 2006

WATERS DARK AND DEEP

*One New Orleans Family's Rescue
Amid the Devastation of Hurricane Katrina*

KATIE THOMAS

Cold Spring Press

Cold Spring Press

P.O. Box 284
Cold Spring Harbor, NY 11724
E-mail: Jopenroad@aol.com

ISBN 1-59360-079-8
Library of Congress Control No. 2005938368
– All Rights Reserved –
Printed in the United States of America

Front cover photo © Rick Wilking/Reuters/Corbis. Photo of Maj. Steven Trisler on p. 1 and in photo insert section by Robert Mecea © 2005 Newsday, Inc., reprinted with permission. Photos from the children's shelter in Baton Rouge courtesy of Brent Broussard. Photos of the reunion are courtesy of Paul Burke. All other photos are courtesy of Katie Thomas.

The title of this book is taken from John Milton's *Paradise Lost:*
"The rising world of waters dark and deep."

For more information about this book, please visit
www.watersdarkanddeep.com.

CONTENTS

To my mother, Betsy Holland, and my father, Mark Thomas

ACKNOWLEDGMENTS

Waters Dark and Deep grew out of my reporting on Hurricane Katrina for Newsday. I'd like to thank Newsday's National Editor, Robert Tiernan, for assigning me to the story, as well as photographer Robert Mecea, who traveled with me to New Orleans and was able to communicate the suffering that we witnessed in ways my own words could not.

The only part of this story I saw with my own eyes was the scene on Interstate 10, when I stumbled upon Major Steven Trisler as he was trying to figure out what to do with these seven kids. As a result, I'm indebted to everyone who shared their lives with me and helped me recreate the dramatic events of that week. Thanks go especially to Catrina Williams and Felecia Love, who invited me into their lives for a week in San Antonio and agreed to share some of their most painful memories. All of the mothers, their spouses and extended family agreed to talk at a time when they had far more pressing matters to attend to. For that, I am grateful.

In addition to the families themselves, I'd also like to thank all of the rescuers, volunteers, social workers and health-department employees who not only patiently answered my questions, but often agreed to dig up records that helped the story come alive. Appreciation in that department goes especially to Alicia Zumbrum, Larry Upchurch, and Charles Pickett at the National Center for Missing and Exploited Children.

Newsday's Long Island Editor, Sandy Keenan, deserves thanks for giving me the time to write this book. Steve Wick, my editor, served as a great advocate. I don't write anything important without submitting it to the legendary Harvey Aronson, and this time was no exception. Thanks to Harvey and Irene Virag for their help. Others who provided support and advice include Lori and Bill Kelly, Ann Givens, Indrani Sen, Andrew Smith,

Joe Haberstroh, and my stepfather, Mark Drnek. And if it weren't for Joie Tyrrell, the hardest working mom in journalism, I wouldn't have been able to write this book at all.

I would also like to acknowledge my publisher, Jonathan Stein of Cold Spring Press, who gave me a chance and offered patient, consistent advice throughout the writing of the book.

Finally, I'd like to thank my fiancé, Alex Mincek, for his love, support and patience.

On August 29, 2005, one of the most powerful hurricanes in recorded history ripped through New Orleans. Hurricane Katrina flooded 80 percent of the city and forced a half million people to flee. The exodus tore husbands from wives, sisters from brothers, and thousands of children from their mothers and fathers. This is the story of one of those families.

Chapter One
"A MATTER OF LIFE AND DEATH"

Catrina Williams looked out her window that Thursday morning, the first day of September, and wondered if the water had something to do with it.

As it lapped below her second-story window, the water reflected the sun's rays and seemed to send them right into the apartment. She couldn't believe how hot it was.

Her four-month-old son, Da'Roneal, wouldn't stop fussing, even though she had long since stripped him down to his bare bottom. Her six-year-old, De'Monté, tried to keep cool by holding a small, battery-powered fan to his face. "But that wasn't even working," she said.

Catrina's younger sister, Felecia Love, wasn't having much better luck. Her one-year-old, Ty're, had broken out in a heat rash. And he wouldn't sleep, no matter how much Felecia rocked.

Zarione, who at two wasn't tall enough to reach the windowsill, didn't understand why they couldn't go home to their apartment just across the street.

"Wanna go? Wanna go?" Zarione kept asking.

"We gotta stay," Felecia answered. "We can't go."

Maybe it was the fact that the water wasn't budging. Maybe it was because the meat had spoiled. Maybe it was the fussing and arguing, which the family had managed to keep at bay until now.

And maybe it was the heat.

Whatever the reason, soon after the household awoke that Thursday morning, everyone – not just Felecia and Catrina but their father, Adrian Love, and Catrina's husband, Darryl Williams – decided they'd had enough.

Three days after Hurricane Katrina crashed through their city, drowning their New Orleans block in about five feet of water, everyone decided Thursday would be their last day at 3223 Third Street.

"We're getting out of here," Catrina told herself as she packed a bag. "We're getting out of here."

In the beginning, the mood inside Catrina's two-bedroom apartment had the feel of a campout.

Adrian, the only one in the family with a car, had decided against leaving the city, opting instead to weather the hurricane with Catrina and Darryl. He came prepared, bringing not only a radio but also a battery-powered television set, candles, a miniature grill and several shopping bags full of chicken, pork and hamburger meat.

At 48, Adrian had seen many hurricanes blow through New Orleans – including the brutal Betsy and Camille in the 1960s – but the city had always survived.

"I don't think it's gonna get really bad," Felecia remembers him saying. Reassured, she cancelled her own plans to leave and decided to spend the storm at Catrina's.

When the clouds parted Monday afternoon, it appeared their father had been right. Aside from some downed trees, a quick walk around the neighborhood showed several buildings had come through with the equivalent of a few scrapes and bruises. There was still no electricity, but no matter. It would come back.

While Adrian grilled pork chops and hamburgers on the balcony, the sisters talked by candlelight and watched as their children played late into the night. It was almost like old times, Catrina and Felecia keeping house in the same apartment, their children more like siblings than cousins.

Almost, that is, except for the cold, dark space that lay between them, the space the sisters carefully avoided each time they were together. Like a child who never dangles a hand below the bed for fear of the monsters lurking beneath, the sisters rarely stepped inside that space.

If they did, both feared it might unleash feelings each had been trying for more than a year to suppress.

On Tuesday, the water arrived, not in a rush but a trickle. Still, brick by brick – at a pace too slow for the naked eye to detect – it rose. When it covered the cars in the parking lot, the family debated what to do.

Outside, people were floating on whatever they could find. "Some people were floating on mattresses and sofas," Felecia said. "I didn't know mattresses could float. I didn't know sofas could float."

If the water rose any higher, the plan was to pry Catrina's doors from their hinges and float away. But with Darryl the only one of the group that could swim, the solution was far from ideal.

Besides, the water was looking increasingly foul. By Thursday, it smelled like a sewer. "Sewer mixed with a dead rat," Felecia said. Pools of oil swirled on the surface, and she saw rats and snakes swimming in the water.

That morning, they realized, staying in the apartment wasn't an option. De'Monté had developed a bad stomachache, leading Catrina to wonder if the heat had spoiled what little meat they had left.

Then the family ran out of bread and water. Da'Roneal was down to just a few bottles of formula, and now Catrina was faced with the prospect of having nothing at all to put in his bottle.

Felecia kept looking outside. "I mean, just knowing that you cannot even get out, you can't even get on ground. I was just trying to hold it together," she said. "I was just trying to hold it together."

With swimming out of the question and staying put unacceptable, the family looked to the skies. For days, Darryl, Adrian and other men in the three-story apartment building had been climbing up to the roof, trying to flag down helicopters with white t-shirts and sheets.

On Thursday, Catrina took matters into her own hands. "I'm like, 'You know what? My kids can't stay like this,'" she said. "I don't care what helicopter, as soon as I see a helicopter I'm going to flag it down."

In the beginning she had no luck. The helicopters were too high, or else they were on their way somewhere else, such as the elementary school nearby that was sheltering hundreds of people.

The sun was already high in the sky when a low-flying helicopter finally spotted her. Catrina leaned her hefty frame out the window and showed the pilot her baby. He waved to acknowledge her and signaled upward.

She understood. Get on the roof.

As Catrina held up Da'Roneal, a neighbor, Marcie Alexander, was also leaning out the window of her apartment down the hall. "I was waving my hands. He saw me," said Marcie, who like Catrina and Felecia was increasingly worried about her child, two-year-old Gabrielle. "He said 'Come upstairs. Come upstairs,' and I'm like 'okay, okay.'"

Within minutes, the mothers of 3223 Third Street crowded onto the third-floor balcony and peered up at the roof, which loomed three feet over their heads.

Catrina, Felecia, and Marcie were there, and so were two others. Keyshawn Carter cradled her two-year-old girl, Dejahney. Yowanda Byrd held her son, two-year-old Leewood Moore, Jr.

Five mothers, seven children. De'Monté, at six, was the oldest. The rest were still in diapers.

The helicopter thumped on the roof, its rotors making so much noise that the mothers had to yell to be understood. They waited on the balcony, while on the roof the men shouted to the helicopter pilot.

Minutes passed, and Catrina began to worry that the pilot had changed his mind. "What's going on? What's the holdup?" she asked.

Then Paul Riley, the building's maintenance man, leaned over the edge of the roof and delivered the news.

The helicopters were only rescuing children.

"When they said that I just, I just cracked up," Catrina said. "What do you mean you want kids only? I'm like oh no, I'm not letting my kids go."

The rest of the mothers were equally resolute.

"They ain't gonna take our children, they ain't gonna take our children," Keyshawn remembers crying. "That's what we was telling them."

As the pilot waited, several of the men pleaded with the women to listen to reason.

"Sweetheart, you gonna have to let 'em go," Adrian told Catrina. "This is a matter of a life or death situation. They ain't gonna survive out here."

The mothers told Paul to ask the pilot where he was taking the children. After a moment's consultation, he returned. The children's final destination was a place called Overleaf, Texas. The pilot promised to return within 25 minutes to collect the mothers.

Keyshawn's baby went first. "She was wondering what was going on," the mother recalled. As Keyshawn lifted her to Paul, Dejahney began to cry. "She saw my face and I looked at her. And we both started crying hard."

The wind from the helicopter's rotors made the handoffs even more difficult. "I was scared he was gonna drop her," Keyshawn said. "He had a hard time getting them."

Finally, Catrina gave in. "I put my selfishness to the side and I said well, all right. And I let 'em go." Darryl took Da'Roneal and passed him to Paul. De'Monté went, too, so quickly that Catrina never had a chance to hug him goodbye.

Felecia also relented. "This is the best thing to do," she told herself. Besides, these pilots are professionals. If they said they were

17

coming back for the mothers, they were coming back for the mothers. "They weren't just anybody. They were the helicopter people. So I just let 'em go. I just let 'em go."

Ty're giggled as she passed him to Paul. Zarione cried.

But Felecia refused to say goodbye. It's a trick she says she's learned since becoming a mother.

"I don't tell them 'bye, because if I tell them 'bye they're gonna start crying," she said. "I don't like to let them know I'm gone. They just look around" and she's gone.

But was there another reason why Felecia refused to say goodbye? Only a year earlier, Catrina and Felecia had lived through the unthinkable. Now, was saying goodbye to another child – a toddler, at that – too hard?

If that was the case, Felecia didn't say.

"I just gave them a kiss, and passed them up," she said.

At the last moment, the mother of a learning disabled boy who lived in another section of the building convinced the pilot to let her on. She jumped in, and the helicopter whirled away.

Catrina and Felecia stared at the sky and told each other it would only be 25 minutes before they saw their babies again. Then the mothers – some who had never met before – collapsed into each other and cried.

They had no idea that there was no such place as Overleaf, Texas.

They had no idea that three tense days would pass before any of them would see their children again.

Chapter Two
THE LEGEND OF DE'MONTÉ LOVE

Catrina and Felecia had just lived through one of the worst natural disasters in American history.

Although the hurricane had slowed by the time it made landfall at around 6:10 a.m. local time on Monday, it was no late-summer squall. Packing sustained winds of 125 miles per hour, Hurricane Katrina hit New Orleans as a powerful Category 3 storm.

As emergency preparations officials and hurricane trackers watched Katrina churn toward land Saturday and Sunday, many of them feared that this could be the "Big One," a hurricane that had the power to overwhelm New Orleans' aging levee system and fill the bowl-shaped city with water. Such a hurricane had long topped emergency officials' lists of major natural hazards, on par with a major earthquake in California or along the New Madrid, Missouri fault line.

By the time the storm was over, nearly everyone realized those fears had been realized. Hurricane Katrina would eventually cause the displacement of up to a million people – four times as many people as were uprooted during the San Francisco earthquake in 1906.

At the moment that the sisters watched their children fly away – noon on Thursday, September 1 – the city had been without power for more than three days. Water inundated not only the sisters' Central City neighborhood, a blighted, desperately poor section of town about a dozen blocks west of the Superdome, but more than 80 percent of the city.

In a poll conducted a year earlier, emergency preparedness officials had discovered that as many as 150,000 New Orleans city residents would not evacuate if ordered. Yet somehow, the droves of people caught in Katrina's wake seemed to take local, state and federal officials by surprise. Not until that Thursday were the first buses arriving at the Superdome to evacuate the estimated 25,000 people who had taken refuge in the arena the city set aside as a shelter.

On that day, federal officials just seemed to be learning about the misery at the New Orleans Convention Center, where another 20,000 people had been living, many without food, water or medical aid, for days.

On the streets that were dry, firefighters without working hydrants watched as flames engulfed entire buildings and then spread down the block. Looters cleaned luxury shops of their contents and shots rang through the city. Police officers resigned en masse. Two committed suicide. Many who stayed on the job roamed the city in packs, concerned as much about their own survival as maintaining order. City paramedics carried personal handguns.

And on virtually every rooftop, tens of thousands of people like Catrina and Felecia waved sheets and shirts and socks and towels at the swarms of helicopters that circled above. Although the Coast Guard's helicopters were the first in the air, their counterparts in the Army, Navy, and the New Orleans Police Department soon joined the pilots. In the flooded sections of town, rescuers pulled the stranded not only from rooftops but highway overpasses and even the tops of trees.

"It's hard to explain," said Lt. Taylor Carlisle, a public affairs officer for the Coast Guard's New Orleans Air Station, which alone assisted in the rescue of more than 8,000 people. "There were so many people on roofs that you could spend all day on one block and not be done."

Because there was no air traffic control directing the flights, pilots were often left on their own to decide whom to rescue first. Coast Guard C-130 and P-3 Orion planes flew overhead, letting pilots know about high-priority rescues such as nursing homes and hospitals. The communications planes also told the pilots where to drop off the evacuees. Sometimes it was a grassy cloverleaf at the intersection of Interstate 10 and Causeway Boulevard. Other times it was Lakefront Airport in the east of town. Later in the week, it was the Louis Armstrong International Airport in Kenner, west of the city.

The women of 3223 Third Street were far from the only parents to hand their children to helicopter pilots.

Rhenda Hodnett, assistant director of program development for Louisiana's Department of Social Services, said the state's hurricane evacuation plan made no special plans for children. However, officials in her department quickly realized that droves of children were likely to be separated from their parents and set up a special children-only shelter in Baton Rouge, the state capitol.

The fact that helicopter pilots would ask for young children – including even babies like Da'Roneal – without allowing their mothers to accompany them baffled Dr. Erin Brewer, medical director for the Office of Public Health in the Louisiana Department of Health and Hospitals.

"I've imagined different scenarios," Brewer said. "Maybe the pilot and the people on the helicopter don't have any children of their own. Maybe they're young and they just wanted to get people out of there. But even that – you still have to think, gosh, we're not doing a very good job of combining military skills and expertise with humanitarian response. That's one of the huge lessons here that we need to learn."

In the chaos and immediacy of such an overwhelming disaster, Carlisle said, separating children from their parents couldn't be helped. "It was a balance issue," she said. "The priority are children and elderly and families, and so if you can only fit the kids in, we take the kids and then you grab one or two adults to care for those children. Our main priority was the preservation of human life."

Although the seven children weren't the only kids torn from their parents during Hurricane Katrina, they were unforgettable to the dozens of rescue workers and volunteers who cared for them.

Maybe it was because there were so many of them. Maybe it was because they were so young. Maybe it was because they were some of the first children to be separated from their parents in those early, topsy-turvy days.

In a horrified country desperate for a scrap of good news, the tale of these seven children plucked from the terror of New Orleans spread from rescue workers to volunteers to state officials, and finally to the press. Like any good word-of-mouth yarn, the story soon outgrew the bounds of truth. By the time the media picked it up, it had become one of the first legends of Hurricane Katrina.

As the story would be told over the next few weeks, rescue workers found little De'Monté abandoned amid the filth and chaos of Interstate 10 and Causeway Boulevard, holding his four-month-old brother in his arms as he kept watch over the five toddlers that surrounded him. That story – and the children's incredible reunification on a tarmac in San Antonio – ran in dozens of papers, from the *Los Angeles Times* to the *Houston Chronicle* to the daily newspaper of Budapest, Hungary.

Catrina was interviewed on Good Morning America.

In a telethon that was broadcast on all major networks September 9, Cameron Diaz mentioned little De'Monté by name. "If a six-year-old boy can be a leader that saves lives, so can you," she said.

That image of De'Monté Love, left to care for six babies on Interstate 10, came to symbolize the chaos of New Orleans in the aftermath of Hurricane Katrina.

Newspaper columnists eulogized him. "In a sea of helpless victims, while heartier adults dithered or complained, Deamonte (sic) found the guts and fortitude to take care of himself, his family and friends," wrote columnist Kathleen Parker, in an op-ed piece that ran in newspapers around the country.

"If this story doesn't move you, I don't know what would," a blogger wrote on one of the dozens of websites that linked to stories about De'Monté. "Read it and try not to cry."

The true story is no less heroic.

The children, it turns out, were not abandoned by the side of the road, but in fact – like an old-fashioned bucket brigade – were lovingly passed from one set of arms to the next. Along the way, the plight of these seven little children managed to pierce even the toughest of skins. In the midst of a sea of human suffering, where even basic needs like food and medical care were hard to come by, rescue workers who had seen it all stopped what they were doing to care for these kids.

On Interstate 10, the children met Major Steven Trisler of the U.S. Army, a soldier who had been awake for 36 hours and was facing the nearly impossible task of bringing in enough buses to evacuate the city. Trisler, an 18-year veteran of the Army who had served in Afghanistan, was more than 500 miles from his own two children in San Antonio when a young woman came to him in desperation. Seven children from her apartment building had flown, motherless, on the helicopter with her. With two of her own children to care for, she needed help.

By the time the woman – he would later learn her name was Shawn Jackson – walked up to him that Thursday afternoon, Trisler had "dealt with every situation in the world." But there was something about this one. "You can't sew the guy's arm up. You can't go back and get that person's mom off of a roof. But you have to take care of these kids right now. That's what has to happen."

After Trisler placed the kids in the care of paramedics, the children met Pat Coveney, Raymond Massie and Brian Sizemore – three ambulance workers who had been speeding their trucks back and forth between I-10 and Baton Rouge for a dozen hours. Back home in

Houston, Massie and Sizemore work for Coveney's ambulance company, which specializes in transporting premature babies. They've seen a lot. But again, there was something about those kids.

Massie and Sizemore carefully strapped the children into their seats and wrapped them in towels to keep them warm in the air-conditioned ambulance. Then Coveney shut the doors. "That's when reality set in for me," Coveney said. "I've done this a long time, and you know I can honestly say that was the hardest thing. When I shut the doors on that ambulance, thinking, here's these kids and where's their parents? Did their parents leave 'em?"

Once in Baton Rouge, Coveney and his men turned the children over to the care of employees of Louisiana's Department of Health and Hospitals. By Thursday, morale was low at the department's emergency operations center. Conditions in New Orleans were turning deadlier by the hour, and yet there seemed to be little anyone could do. They listened, powerless, as the radio reported that patients were dying in hospitals as they waited to be rescued.

"We had spent the week sending ambulances in and having them be turned away," recalled Dr. Brewer. "We were just so upset and frustrated and feeling so really, honestly, helpless."

Then the children arrived. Although De'Monté and the toddlers had just lived through an unimaginable calamity – and quite possibly lost their parents for good – none of them dwelled on the tragedy. Within minutes, the children were playing, drawing pictures with workers and running around the room. "They were so relatively unscathed and we were all just so frazzled and upset," Brewer said. "They just lure you in."

When the kids moved to the children's shelter across town, they continued to leave a mark on nearly everyone they met.

The children instantly bonded with a group from the Big Buddy Program in Baton Rouge, an after-school program that serves underprivileged kids. With most of the children in diapers and some just learning to talk, the children were far younger than the kids the group normally works with. After a day of being passed from one set of rescuers to another, the children grabbed onto these Big Buddy workers – most of whom were in their 20s and had no children of their own – and wouldn't let go. By the time the children drifted to sleep in their cots late Thursday night, the Big Buddy crew was hooked.

In the middle of the night, Derrick Robertson, a 27-year-old director of the group's Middle School Initiatives program, called co-worker Jodi McKenzie. She had taken a picture of De'Monté with her camera phone earlier in the day. Would she mind e-mailing it?

Finally, the children met Joe Newport, the retired chief of the Terre Haute, Indiana police force and a member of Team Adam, an elite squad created by the National Center for Missing and Exploited Children who are deployed around the country to help in missing-kids cases.

By the time he arrived at the children's shelter that Friday, Newport had become an expert at finding missing boys and girls. Now, he found the tables had turned. Sitting in his makeshift office in the hallway of the Louisiana State University field house, Newport could watch the kids as they played with Derrick and the other Big Buddy workers.

This time, he had to find the parents.

As an army of rescue workers and volunteers cared for their children, Catrina, Felecia and the rest of the mothers embarked on an ordeal of their own. Five hours would pass before another helicopter would land on their roof, but when it dropped them off at Lakefront Airport, their children were nowhere to be found. Another helicopter ride Friday morning took them to Louis Armstrong International Airport, where they boarded planes to San Antonio.

Along the way, Catrina worried that people would think she had abandoned De'Monté and Da'Roneal, not understanding the desperate decision she had been forced to make. She tried to tell herself that no one could mistake the chubby Da'Roneal for an abandoned baby. "My son may be slim but my baby is fat," she said. "You know, he eats."

As for De'Monté, she prayed that he would remember the details she had drilled into him for years. Catrina is a diabetic, and always worried that if she passed out on the street, De'Monté wouldn't know what to do. So as soon as he could talk, she made him memorize his name, his parents' names, his address, his phone number. "I don't try to grow him up fast but I try to make him so he understands. So, you know, if I'm not around or whatever, nobody could just tell him anything."

Felecia also worried about her babies, though she tried hard not to let it show. Ty're was such a happy child, she had a feeling he would be fine. But she worried about Zarione, who was given to fits of crying. "I was just trying to keep it together," she said.

And for both women, there was something else, something rarely spoken but always simmering just below the surface.

Not again, each woman said to herself. Not again.

Chapter Three
THE FIRE BEFORE THE FLOOD

Some grandparents claim they don't play favorites.

Not Rosemary Joseph.

Ro'Neal Love was his grandma's "little heart," an affectionate two-year-old who preferred the company of adults.

When Felecia would bring her children to Rosemary's house, one-year-old Zarione would run off to play with her cousins. But not Ro'Neal. "Mama, I love you," Ro'Neal would tell his grandma as he climbed onto her bed and gave her a kiss.

And if Rosemary was the one paying a visit on Felecia, Ro'Neal would beg her to take him along when it came time to leave. "I'm gonna get my shoes and my jacket," she recalled him saying as he headed toward the door. He had trouble saying "jacket."

Many nights, Ro'Neal would convince Felecia to dial his grandmother's house so he could say goodnight.

The night of May 26, 2004, was one of those times.

"Grandma, I love you," Ro'Neal said, in the way of a two-year-old still mastering his vowels and consonants.

"I love you too, Ro'Neal," she answered.

Then he asked one of his favorite questions. "You got some money?"

"No," Rosemary answered with a chuckle. "Does your mama got some money?"

Ro'Neal delivered the punch line with gusto: "My momma don't got no money."

Rosemary hung up the phone with a smile on her face. She had no idea she would never hear Ro'Neal's voice again.

On the morning of May 27, 2004, Catrina was bone tired.

She had been working the graveyard shift at her job as a cook at the Quick n' Easy, a deli and gas station near the Louis Armstrong International Airport in Kenner, a suburb west of New Orleans. Midnight to 8 a.m. was no picnic, but getting there made it even worse. Without a car, the 18-mile commute took three hours – aboard three buses – from her apartment in east New Orleans to the deli.

Sometimes, Catrina got so tired that she convinced Darryl to come with her, just so she didn't fall asleep. "I used to wear myself out," she said.

So it was late morning by the time Catrina returned to the one-bedroom apartment she shared with Felecia. Although the apartment was tiny, the sisters had carved out separate living quarters for each family. Felecia, at 22 the younger of the two, and her three children – Ro'Neal, Zarione, and baby Ty're – lived in the bedroom. Catrina, who was 26, claimed the living room for herself, Darryl and De'Monté.

Felecia and Catrina's sister, Alisha, lived upstairs in a two-bedroom apartment with her husband and two girls.

A few minutes after Catrina walked through her door, Alisha popped her head in. Did De'Monté want to come upstairs and play with her girls? Catrina gladly agreed, and fell into bed.

The phone woke her several hours later. It was Alisha. De'Monté and her daughter, Gerall'ycia, were fighting over a toy. Alisha had to go to work soon anyway. Could she send De'Monté back down? Catrina said okay, and hung up the phone.

De'Monté walked through the door a few minutes later.

"Are you hungry? Do you want a snack?" Catrina asked.

"Yeah," De'Monté answered.

"Then straighten up." Catrina pointed at the toys that were strewn across the carpet. "Straighten up and Mama's gonna give you a treat."

As he cleaned, Catrina fell back asleep.

On her way to work as a housekeeper at a gas station, Alisha – who was 23 and the middle sibling – had a habit of checking in on her sisters before she left to catch the bus. When she cracked open the door, Catrina and De'Monté were both asleep on the bed. Alisha tiptoed past them and tapped on Felecia's door. She visited for a while with Felecia and the kids, then kissed them goodbye.

"Something told me, 'don't go to work,'" Alisha said. "But we really needed the money, so I went."

Catrina woke to the sound of Felecia, yelling.

"Boy, no you didn't," she shouted.

Catrina jumped out of bed.

A fire – small, still – licked the carpet near the bed. De'Monté held a lighter in his hand.

As Felecia ran into her bedroom, De'Monté followed her.

Catrina lunged toward him, intent on scolding him. But when she turned her head and looked at the fire again, it had risen several inches. The flames were now up to her knee, and they were spreading to the bed.

"What am I going to do? What am I going to do?" Catrina asked herself, trying to keep the panic at bay.

The building's apartments had no fire extinguishers, a fact that had been the source of an ongoing argument between Alisha and the landlady, who the sisters said had a stack of them in her apartment but hadn't gotten around to passing them out.

"Come out here. Y'all come out," Catrina shouted to Felecia, who was still in the bedroom with De'Monté and her kids.

"I can't," Felecia answered. One look at the door told Catrina why. It was covered in flames.

"The fire, it spread so quick," Felecia recalled. "I just turned my back and it spread so quick."

By this time, a thick black smoke had filled the apartment.

Choking, Catrina felt her way to the front door.

In the hallway, she pounded on doors.

Alerted by her cries and the smell of smoke, neighbors poured out of their apartments. Some tried to get in – even breaking the back window – but were pushed back by the heat.

"The fire was so bad that the door was hot. I couldn't get back in," Catrina said.

Down the street, neighbor Rita Shaw smelled the smoke and ran toward the apartment building. As she got close to the gate, a woman ran toward her, holding a baby who was covered in soot. His skin had blistered in the fire. "I screamed and told her to give me the baby," Shaw recalled.

The fire engines – ten in all – arrived a few minutes later. Catrina stood outside the building and sobbed. Her nightgown had burned to rags, but she didn't care. As she took stock of her surroundings, she saw that somehow Felecia, De'Monté and Zarione had gotten out of the apartment. Ty're was the baby that Shaw now held in her arms.

But where was Ro'Neal?

Then Catrina noticed that Felecia was crying.

Catrina and Felecia tried to run back into the apartment, but the firefighters wouldn't let them in.

"I'm looking at the men like – I know they're good men – but I'm like, please go in there, try to get him," Catrina recalled.

"You can't do anything," they told her. "He's gone."

The firefighters finally found Ro'Neal lying on the floor, between two beds. He was dead.

Although a front-page article in the *Times-Picayune* reported that a match near the bed started the fire, Catrina said De'Monté later told fire investigators that he had tried to burn Darryl's video game console with a lighter.

The apartment had no smoke detector, firefighters told the *Times-Picayune*.

Ty're suffered second-degree burns, and the fire singed the back of De'Monté's head. It took 30 firefighters to bring the blaze under control. When it was all over, the fire gutted the sisters' apartment and caused major damage to another.

The family gathered that night at the hospital, where the children were being treated for their burns. Catrina, too, had been admitted because of shortness of breath. At first, Alisha and the others weren't allowed to see Felecia, because she was with her surviving children. When she finally came out, she could barely talk.

"I miss my baby," she said. "I tried, I tried."

That night, the Red Cross paid for the sisters to stay in adjoining hotel rooms. Only a door separated her from Felecia, but Catrina couldn't bring herself to open it. Because De'Monté had started the fire, she felt Ro'Neal's death was her fault. She tried to imagine her sister, grieving on the other side, but she couldn't open the door.

Ro'Neal was laid to rest one week later in "Angel's Rest," a corner of Metairie's Lake Lawn Cemetery dedicated to babies. They buried him in a white coffin covered with feathers, a box that seemed impossibly small, even for a two-year-old boy.

His gravestone is simple. "Roneal Love," it reads. "Sept. 18, 2001 – May 27, 2004."

Catrina and Felecia made small talk at his wake, but neither brought up the fire. It was just too soon. As the months passed, the fire and Ro'Neal's death lay between them. Rather than talk about it – rather than enter that cold, dark space – they drifted apart.

Rosemary noticed the rift but felt powerless to mend it. Although Felecia never came out and said it, "I think every time she looked at

Monté, she thought about her child not being there and why he wasn't there."

Rosemary tried to talk to her daughter about it. "Monté is only a baby," she would tell Felecia. "He didn't know no better."

Felecia wasn't mad at De'Monté. She wasn't mad at Catrina, either. But one sentence kept cycling through her head, and it was hard to dismiss it.

"He's here, my baby's not," she would think. "He's here, my baby's not."

The shadow cast by Ro'Neal's death spread beyond Catrina and Felecia. Other adults found it tough to be around each other.

"I lost interest in celebrating holidays. It wasn't the same," Rosemary said. "Even though I still had my other grandchildren, Neal wasn't there."

Felecia couldn't bear to be alone, so she moved in with Alisha, even though she still lived in the same building, one floor above Catrina and Felecia's old apartment.

They took roundabout routes to avoid passing the gutted apartment, but the smell of smoke hung everywhere, even weeks after the fire.

At first, Felecia only slept during the day. "At night, we couldn't get her to sleep," Alisha said. "It was such a shock."

Ro'Neal's death took its toll on Catrina, as well.

After the fire Catrina, Darryl and De'Monté moved in with one of Rosemary's sisters. Whenever she left the house, she had panic attacks. "I insulated myself to myself. I didn't want to be bothered by nobody," Catrina said. "I just felt like, what is there outside? There's nothing outside."

She grieved for Ro'Neal like a son. "He wasn't my child but he was my nephew. And we were all staying in an apartment," Catrina said. "And it hurt me to see my sister with her two kids and knowing that she had three."

Sam Adams, Catrina's supervisor at the Quick n' Easy, noticed the change. Her legendary sense of humor – the one that made her a favorite among the regular customers – disappeared. "She was quieter than before," Adams said. Sometimes, he would try to make her laugh by playing one of her favorite songs – "Somebody's Gettin' on My Nerves," by Salt n' Pepa.

Catrina would smile, and say something polite. But she wasn't the same.

The children couldn't stop talking about Ro'Neal's death. Sometimes, in the middle of an ordinary conversation, De'Monté would blurt out a memory from the fire.

"He would talk about when they were trying to get out, the last person he looked back and saw was Ro'Neal behind him," Rosemary said.

Concerned about what type of effect the memory would have on the child, Rosemary discouraged De'Monté from raising the topic. "Monté, we've got to let it go," she'd tell him.

One day, four-year-old Gerall'ycia gazed at the wall in Rosemary's home dedicated to photos of Ro'Neal.

"I wanna go where Neal's at," Gerall'ycia said. "He's up there in the sky and I want to go."

"No, you don't," Rosemary said. "We all miss him and we all love him, but we just gonna always have him in our heart."

As time passed, the rift between Catrina and Felecia narrowed. After the New Year, Darryl got a job making furniture, and Catrina discovered she was pregnant. With the baby coming and a steady income, they decided to get their own apartment. When the baby was born, Catrina named him after Darryl and Ro'Neal, combining the two names into one. Da'Roneal was a happy, healthy baby, and after his arrival, some of Catrina's good nature returned.

Around the same time, Felecia found some stability of her own. Since February 2005, she had been pulling in good money as a waitress at the Court of Two Sisters, a high-end restaurant in the French Quarter known for its sumptuous brunches. That month, she moved into an apartment across the street from Catrina.

The neighborhood the sisters moved to, however, was far from ideal.

In New Orleans, poverty is as much a part of the fabric of life as Mardi Gras or red beans and rice. Yet Central City was poorer still.

Figures from the 2000 Census tell a stark tale.

In 1999, for example, 28 percent of New Orleans residents overall lived below the poverty line, meaning they earned less than $15,000 for a family of three. But in the census tract that included Catrina and Felecia's houses – an area of roughly 40 blocks – more than half lived in poverty.

In New Orleans, 28 percent had never finished high school. In Central City, 47 percent never earned a diploma.

Single women headed just under half of New Orleans' homes. But nearly three-quarters of Catrina and Felecia's neighbors lived in households led by single women.

Nearly half of New Orleanians owned their own homes. In Central City, only 22 percent did.

While Hurricane Katrina added a new layer of devastation to the streets of Central City, the neighborhood was in disrepair to begin with.

Rosalind Peychaud, a former Louisiana state representative whose district included Central City, remembers being struck by the neighborhood's destitution while campaigning there in the fall of 2003. From abandoned houses to junked cars to trash-strewn lots, Central City was "an area that you would think people wouldn't choose to live in," Peychaud said.

Many residents live in classic New Orleans "shotgun" homes – long, narrow houses built of cypress in the early 20th century. While the shotguns in some of the city's gentrifying neighborhoods have been lovingly restored, in Central City they creak on their cinderblock foundations. Their once-white walls are gray with the exhaust from passing cars. Windows are broken, and screen doors sag open.

Bars without names sit on many street corners, as do fish shops and po-boy stands.

"It's a blighted neighborhood," said Captain Anthony Cannatella, commanding officer of the Sixth District, which includes Central City.

Catrina's apartment is two blocks from the notorious intersection of Third and Galvez Streets, a corner so popular for drug-dealing that a local gang, 3NG, named itself after it. A few blocks to the west is "Mikey's Garden," a once-empty lot where in 1994 a four-year-old boy was killed in a drive-by shooting. Community organizers renamed the lot after the boy and planted a garden in his memory.

Prostitutes frequent an abandoned house within walking distance of Catrina's apartment. One was killed there not too long ago.

Just across the street from her building is the John W. Hoffman Elementary School, where De'Monté attended kindergarten. Despite years of attempts to improve the school's performance, Hoffman elementary consistently ranked near the bottom of New Orleans' already troubled schools.

In 1999, for example, the school ranked 246th out of New Orleans's 261 elementary schools. That same year, Hoffman received a score of 17 out of a possible 200 points on a state performance test. During the 2003-2004 school year, the state of Louisiana singled Hoffman out as being "academically unacceptable."

Finally, in the spring of 2005, the district threw in the towel. Hoffman elementary would close its doors, and students – including De'Monté – would move to a neighboring elementary school that performed marginally better on state tests.

The school's closing was a blow to community activists like Peychaud, who now heads the Neighborhood Development Foundation, a group that helps low-income families become homeowners. For the past two years, Peychaud had been realizing a dream that had Hoffman Elementary as its anchor.

Hoffman, despite its poor academic performance, was nevertheless a community center that could provide neighbors with a common identity. When Peychaud toured the neighborhood that fall campaign season, she didn't just notice the empty lots and the junked cars. Other details struck her as well – the area had beautiful oak trees, barbershops, and churches – not to mention a clear view of the Superdome and downtown.

"I thought that at some point this must have been a very nice area," said Peychaud.

So beginning in late 2003, Peychaud's group secured financing and built five new homes, which she then sold to low-income families.

As the months passed, Peychaud convinced others to chip in and rebuild the area she named "Hoffman Triangle." The city fixed streetlights that had long been broken, and repaved the streets. It also invested $500,000 in refurbishing Taylor Park, which was next to the elementary school and across from Catrina's apartment.

"What we had hoped for is that there would be a ripple effect of interest," Peychaud said, and other investors would also build in the area. When the district closed Hoffman Elementary, "We were just getting started."

To an outsider, Central City wasn't the ideal place to raise a family. But to Catrina and Felecia, who had spent their lives moving from one poor New Orleans neighborhood to another, it wasn't so bad.

Catrina, especially, liked her apartment, which at $513 a month was a good deal. The apartment, though small, had two bedrooms and wall-to-wall carpets. The stove and refrigerator were new, and – best of all – the apartment was equipped with a fire extinguisher and smoke detector.

"International Apartments," as the building at 3223 Third Street was called, was one of the only apartment buildings in the area. Its

1970s-era concrete façade loomed over the shotgun houses along the block. A chain-link fence surrounded the building, and the gate was connected to an electronic security system, which made Catrina feel safe. If you asked the landlord to fix something, he took care of it.

"It was a beautiful apartment," she said.

Things were starting to get back to normal.

For the first time in months, Felecia said, "I was really happy. Really happy."

When Hurricane Katrina came, the sisters decided to weather the storm – together.

Chapter Four
THE BIG ONE

❀

On Tuesday, August 23 – six days before the hurricane hit New Orleans – meteorologists noticed a knot of low pressure forming over the southeastern Bahamas. They labeled it Tropical Depression 12, or TD-12, for short.

One notch below a tropical storm, a tropical depression is an area of low pressure that's large enough to be plotted on a weather map. When a tropical depression forms, winds begin to swirl around the area, drawing in warm, moist air. The more warm air the storm takes in, the faster the winds blow.

The wind speeds increased overnight, and by Wednesday, August 24, TD-12 had earned the right to be given a proper name: Tropical Storm Katrina, the eleventh named storm of the 2005 hurricane season. The rest of the day, Katrina continued to gather strength as it moved across the Bahamas and toward Florida.

At 6:30 a.m. on Friday, the storm's winds reached speeds of 75 miles per hour. Tropical Storm Katrina was now a hurricane.

That morning, Katrina made contact for the first time with U.S. soil, striking between Hallandale Beach and North Miami Beach, Florida, and packing winds of 80 miles per hour. As it moved southwest across the tip of the peninsula, the storm knocked out power to 1.3 million Florida customers, and killed at least 11 people.

Like any storm, it lost strength as it moved over land and toward the Gulf of Mexico. But once Katrina reached open water, the storm fed on the Gulf's supply of warm, moist air and intensified again.

On that day, Louisiana Governor Kathleen Babineaux Blanco declared a state of emergency. "Hurricane Katrina poses an imminent threat to the state of Louisiana, carrying severe storms, high winds, and torrential rain that may cause flooding and damage to private property and public facilities," the declaration read.

But despite the warning, many New Orleanians – including Catrina and Felecia – didn't pay much attention.

In a city famous for its jazz funerals and hurricane cocktails, a mix of fatalism and bravado prevailed among its citizens. Sure, there were memories of Hurricane Betsy in 1965, which flooded many parts of the city and led to 76 deaths. And many remembered Camille, the Category 5 storm that hit New Orleans four years later, battering the coast with winds approaching 190 miles per hour.

There was also dark humor about the "Big One" – a major hurricane that had the power to burst the levees protecting New Orleans from Lake Pontchartrain and the Mississippi River and fill the city with water. In fact, the "Big One" was more than a joke.

For years, emergency preparedness officials at every level of government knew that the city's levees, when they were built in the 1960s, had not been designed to withstand anything beyond a Category 3 hurricane. Although there were plans to study beefing up the city's protection in the event of a major storm, everyone knew that doing so would cost billions of dollars – money that the city and the state didn't have.

In June 2002, the *New Orleans Times-Picayune* published "Washing Away," an investigative series that painted what must have then seemed like a doomsday scenario – if a major hurricane hit the city, the paper reported, most of New Orleans would be flooded. Tens of thousands would be trapped in their homes and rooftops. Thousands more would die. New Orleans as we know it would be gone, the paper warned.

But to many who lived in the city, the fear of the "Big One" was blunted by the more run-of-the-mill hurricanes that regularly blew through the Big Easy. Storms came and went along the Gulf Coast, so much so that weathering them had become a kind of badge of honor. Between 1851 and 2004, 49 hurricane-strength storms hit the coast, but only 18 reached the status of "major hurricane." Only four were Category 4 storms, and only one – Camille – was a Category 5.

At 4 a.m. on the morning of Saturday, August 27, Hurricane Katrina was still 435 miles from the mouth of the Mississippi River. With top winds reaching 115 miles per hour, the storm was now a Category 3.

Now, Katrina began to attract more attention. At 10 a.m., the National Weather Service declared a hurricane watch for southeastern Louisiana, which included New Orleans.

Later that day, at Governor Blanco's request, President George W. Bush declared a federal emergency in Louisiana, although he stopped short of ordering a full-scale response to the storm.

That afternoon, Blanco and New Orleans Mayor Ray Nagin held a joint press conference and urged city residents to leave, especially those who lived in low-lying areas.

"Ladies and gentlemen, this is not a test. This is the real deal," Nagin warned. "Board up your homes, make sure you have enough medicine, make sure the car has enough gas. Do all the things you normally do for a hurricane but treat this one differently because it is pointed towards New Orleans."

That evening, Catrina called Felecia at work.

"Pack your stuff, pack your stuff," Catrina said.

"For what?"

"A hurricane's coming."

"Ok," Felecia said. She didn't think it was serious.

Then one of her friends at work walked up to her.

"Where y'all going?"

"I don't know," Felecia answered.

"It's really gonna hit us this time," the friend said.

By the time Felecia got home, the warnings had gotten worse.

So she started packing a bag. Her father, Adrian, was across the street at Catrina's with his car, getting ready to take them out of town.

But as the hours passed, Adrian became less and less worried about the storm. "I don't think it's really gonna hit," Felecia remembers him saying. "We was panicking, but you know he was calm."

While Adrian's fears were receding, Hurricane Katrina was gaining strength. At 1 a.m. on Sunday morning, storm trackers clocked winds at speeds of 145 miles per hour. The storm was now a Category 4.

Six hours later, Katrina loomed 250 miles southeast of the mouth of the Mississippi and was still gaining steam. At 7 a.m., Katrina's sustained winds topped out at 160 miles per hour. For only the second time in the state's recorded history, a Category 5 storm was headed toward the Louisiana coast.

There was no doubt about it: This was the Big One.

The National Hurricane Center's advisory that morning called the storm "potentially catastrophic" and predicted storm surges of 15 to 20 feet along the coast.

At 9:30 a.m., for the first time in city history, the mayor ordered a mandatory evacuation of New Orleans. Tens of thousands of people – an estimated two-thirds of New Orleans' population of half a million people – heeded Nagin's orders. The emptying of New Orleans was the first evacuation of a major city since the Civil War.

Felecia's apartment building was made of brick. Catrina's was concrete.

If they were going to stay in New Orleans, the sisters decided, they'd better do it at Catrina's.

In nearby apartments, other families were making similar calculations. Down the hall from Catrina, Marcie Alexander discovered she'd missed her chance at getting a ride with her sister to Dallas. Without a car of her own, she and her roommate, Yowanda Byrd, decided to ride out the storm. "We might as well just stick it out," Marcie recalls thinking.

Next door to Catrina, Patricia Carter's hurricane plan involved a higher power. She shared the apartment with her daughter, Keyshawn, and her granddaughter, two-year-old Dejahney. "I'm the type of person where I never evacuate," she said. As the storm approached, she decided, "I'm just gonna put my trust in the Lord."

By Sunday night, the nation was holding its collective breath as it tracked Hurricane Katrina's path.

Inside 3223 Third Street, nearly every apartment was full.

And no wonder.

According to the 2000 Census, nearly 60 percent of the people in Catrina and Felecia's neighborhood did not own a car. What's more, in a neighborhood where more than half of families lived below the poverty line, many households relied on public assistance to pay their daily expenses. Hurricane Katrina hit on August 29 – the end of the month. Many families had run out of money to pay for the gas, lodging and food they'd need to evacuate.

Sometimes residents' bravado masked more practical reasons for staying behind. Patricia Carter, for example, later amended her reason for not leaving town. It wasn't just about her faith in the Lord, she said. She didn't have a car, much less enough money to pay for a hotel. "So I really didn't have a choice but stay anyway," she said.

Hurricane planners had long predicted much of the city would not evacuate even if ordered to do so.

In July 2004, officials from the National Weather Service, the U.S. Army Corps of Engineers and 50 other agencies engaged in a hypothetical exercise designed to test the New Orleans area's ability to weather a major storm. "Hurricane Pam," as the fake storm was dubbed, was a Category 3 hurricane that dumped 20 inches of rain on the city. When the exercise was over, officials estimated that such a hurricane would likely trap as many as 300,000 people in the city, many of whom would not have access to transportation.

A follow-up study was planned for the summer of 2005, but was never conducted. Instead, in July, city officials began a public education campaign targeted at New Orleans' poorest residents. On DVDs that were distributed in low-income areas, the message was this: In the event of a major hurricane, the city won't have the resources to evacuate all of its citizens. According to an article in the *Times-Picayune*, city officials estimated then that 134,000 people wouldn't have a way to get out of the city.

The rains began Sunday night.

"I thought it was the end of the world," Catrina said.

The sky was black above Central City's empty streets, punctuated every now and again by lightning. "It just looked like a ghost town," she said. "It looked like it was haunted."

As the winds picked up, Adrian pulled the mattresses off the beds and propped them up against the windows.

Wind-driven rain bashed against the windows, and outside, the family heard crashes and bangs – falling trees, light poles, and who knew what else.

Down the hall, in Marcie's apartment, everyone piled into the bathroom. Marcie and Yowanda sat in the tub with their children. Marcie's cousin and her boyfriend shared the toilet seat.

Later, Marcie ventured into the bedroom and got up the nerve to peek outside. "The house that was next door to the apartments, you could see directly in the house," she said. "The windows were gone, the siding was gone, everything was gone."

Marcie tried adopting a fatalistic attitude, but it did little to ease her fear. "If the winds just take us, they just take us," she told herself.

Sometime in the night, the power went out. Adrian Love lit the candles he had brought for just this occasion. The family listened to the battery-powered radio for a while, and then went to sleep.

Although the rain and tropical storm-force winds had been hitting the city for hours, Hurricane Katrina made landfall in Plaquemines Parish at 6:10 a.m. as a Category 3 storm. The winds had weakened slightly and were now 125 miles per hour.

Four hours later, the storm made landfall again, this time near the border between Louisiana and Mississippi. As it moved northeast over land, it gradually lost power.

On Monday afternoon, the rains in New Orleans finally stopped.

"Daddy," Catrina told Adrian, "I'm so glad it's over with."

Across the country, Americans shared Catrina's relief.

"New Orleans pummeled by hurricane, but avoided the worst," read a headline on a Cox News Service story from that Monday. "New Orleans relieved after storm jogs east," read another on Tuesday in Minnesota's *Saint Paul Pioneer Press*. "Spared again," declared the *St. Petersburg Times*, in Florida.

While Catrina watched the children, Felecia and the others ventured outside. Trees had fallen, and some homes were torn apart. But despite the devastation, there was celebration among those who had survived the storm.

"Everybody was just walking around, just waving at each other," Marcie said.

But even as the residents of Central City rejoiced in having made it through, the radio brought ominous news from elsewhere in the city. As Katrina passed through New Orleans early that morning, the storm surge sent water sloshing over the city's Industrial Canal, flooding parts of the city and the adjacent St. Bernard Parish. Then, later that day, City Hall confirmed reports that the crucial 17th Street canal levee had given way, sending water from Lake Pontchartrain into the city.

By the time the residents of 3223 Third Street ventured outside that evening, several New Orleans neighborhoods were already under several feet of water.

Although Marcie and Felecia said they saw no looting, troublemakers were wreaking havoc not far from Third Street. A few blocks away, a band of looters stole a fleet of limousines from a funeral home and parked them outside the B.W. Cooper public housing projects. Others raided a pawnshop on South Claiborne Avenue and set it on fire.

Also that evening, word spread throughout the building that the police had opened the Winn-Dixie on South Claiborne. With the power likely to be out for days, the rumor went, the police were letting people in to stock up on food.

With a guilty conscience, the women of 3223 Third Street headed to the store.

Patricia Carter prayed to God before she walked through the doors. "Oh Lord, you know I don't want to do this, but on the other hand you know we've got to eat, we've got to survive," she prayed.

Outside the store, police cars guarded the entrance, and officers stood on either side of the doors, maintaining order. Capt. Cannatella, the commanding officer of the police district that includes Central City, said the doors had been pried open by the time police reached the store, but acknowledged that once open, officers let families take supplies.

Inside, Marcie said, the mood wasn't unlike shopping on a busy Sunday afternoon. "Everybody was talking, just like you normally shop," she said. With one exception, that is – some were pulling cash out of the registers.

Yowanda and Marcie hadn't prepared at all for the hurricane. Both received food stamps, and had used them all by the time Katrina blew in. The two brought home smoked sausage, ground meat for hamburgers, cheese, chips and soda. The only bread left was wheat bread – not Marcie's favorite, but she took it anyway.

By the time Patricia arrived, her choices were slimmer: canned tuna and Vienna sausages. "I'm not even into Vienna sausages, either," she said. "But when it comes to that, you'd be surprised what you can be forced to eat."

The water arrived on Tuesday.

When it reached three feet, Catrina and Felecia considered leaving. The Superdome was only 12 blocks to the east. But Adrian advised against it. "See, it will stop," he said.

By nightfall, the water had nearly reached the second floor, forcing the first-floor tenants to take cover with families on the third, and highest, floor. Felecia tried not to panic. "The water could rise to the second floor," she remembered thinking. "If it rises to the second floor, it could rise to the third floor. And then we really gonna be sick."

Catrina wasn't as calm. "I could have dealt with the power being out for a little while," she said. "I could have dealt with a little water."

When the flood engulfed the cars in the parking lot, "That's when I was like, 'Oh Lord, please just help us get out of this.'"

Seen from above, the black, fetid water must have indeed seemed ominous. However, a tour of their neighborhood two months after Hurricane Katrina showed the water line – the filthy border that bisects houses, lampposts and cars after the floods recede – only reached about five feet. An adult might have been able to wade to safety.

In fact Cannatella said several Central City residents did just that.

However, several factors likely combined to make wading through the water seem impossible. First, Cannatella said, the fact that the water covered the cars tricked the eye into believing the water was deeper than it actually was. Many people, he said, mistakenly assume cars are taller than they are.

In addition, even though an adult may be able to safely wade through four to five feet of water, Catrina, Felecia and the other parents would have had to carry the children – most of whom were under two

– over their heads for perhaps a dozen blocks. What's more, the water that filled the streets was polluted with chemicals and gasoline, not to mention dead animals and sewage. Several of the mothers said they saw snakes swimming in the water. Who knows what the parents would have been stepping on as they made their way to safety.

Finally, with the exception of Darryl, none of the adults knew how to swim.

On Wednesday, tempers frayed as panic grew. "It was lots of arguing," Catrina said. "They had a lady upstairs, she was just going off. People was getting disgusted."

Like Catrina, Yowanda was a diabetic. She also suffered from high blood pressure. Several times, she almost passed out in the heat. "Everybody had a little attitude."

Some of their neighbors, in either frustration or boredom, threw paper and clothes into the increasingly foul water. On either Wednesday or Thursday – by this time, the days were flowing into one another – someone set a fire on the second-story balcony.

"I just straight panicked," Catrina said. "I was sitting up there looking at the water like, Lord, I'm about to take my family and jump in the water, because I'm not about to get burned by the fire. Because I know how it feels to be playing around with that."

The fire was doused as its perpetrators sheepishly explained that they were only trying to signal one of the helicopters that were now thumping through the air.

By Thursday, the women of 3223 Third Street were desperate.

So desperate, in fact, they were willing to betray every maternal instinct and do the unthinkable – push a baby, five toddlers and a six-year-old into a helicopter and hope for the best.

For Catrina and Felecia, the decision was especially painful. Only 16 months after Ro'Neal's death, the sisters were again facing the possibility of losing their children.

"That's the part that scared me," Felecia said. "You know, I already went through a tragedy. I can't risk losing these two."

When the helicopter disappeared from the sky, the sisters climbed onto the roof. It began to rain.

Now, they waited.

Chapter Five
ONE BIG MEASLE

❀

Major Steven Trisler couldn't afford to dawdle.

It was Tuesday, August 30, and Tuesdays meant baseball practice.

So at 4 p.m. sharp, he shut down his computer and drove his red pickup truck – a 2005 Silverado, fresh off the dealer's lot – toward home.

Since being transferred to San Antonio two months earlier, home was on a pleasant, upper-middle class street of tract houses in the northeast of town, not too far from his office at the Fort Sam Houston Army base. The neighborhood's respectability embarrassed Trisler a bit. It wasn't really in keeping with his working-class Indiana upbringing, but in San Antonio, $200,000 buys you a nice house. One can't help that, he reasoned.

Lance, his seven-year-old, and Thalia, 4, were busy with homework when Trisler walked through the door. For a couple of weeks now, Trisler had been helping out with Lance's Little League team. Without a particular knack for the game, Trisler had left teaching baseball to the other dads. His job was to make sure the kids were getting along and coming up to bat in the right order. "I'm what I call the dugout babysitter," he said.

After fixing a pre-game snack, Trisler packed a bag for himself and Lance, throwing in balls, mitts, bats, and bottled water. He set them by the door. Around 5:30, the two walked to the porch and laced up their cleats.

Just as they were pulling out of the driveway, Trisler's cell phone rang.

"Ltc Arnold," the screen read. Lieutenant Colonel Edwina Arnold. His boss.

Pack your bags, she said. Plan to be gone for three to 30 days. You're going to New Orleans.

Trisler hung up the phone.

It's about time, he thought.

For nearly a week, Trisler had been watching Hurricane Katrina as it thrashed toward New Orleans and wondering when he would get the call.

As a logistics officer for the U.S. Army, Trisler was used to getting calls like this. Helping with hurricane relief is one of the missions of the Fifth Army, the division of the U.S. Army charged with protecting the western United States from natural or manmade disasters. Fifth Army soldiers are often deployed as backup, providing logistical support to the "doers" – the National Guard, for example, or the Federal Emergency Management Agency.

As Trisler tracked Katrina's path in its early days, he paid close attention to where it might hit. If it made landfall in Alabama and Mississippi, the storm would be the responsibility of the First Army, which is tasked with protecting the United States east of the Mississippi. But if it hit Galveston, Corpus Christi or even western Louisiana, then Trisler knew to expect a phone call.

On Friday, as New Orleans – which straddles both sides of the Mississippi – entered the "cone" of the hurricane's potential path, "I had a funny feeling I was gonna wind up in this mess," Trisler said.

On Saturday, the hurricane picked up strength. Sunday came, and with it the National Weather Service's predictions of a "potentially catastrophic" hit on New Orleans.

On Monday morning, just as the storm was landing on the Gulf Coast, Trisler drove to his office at Fort Sam Houston. "Why didn't I get a call over the weekend?" he wondered.

Maybe it's because I'm new, Trisler thought. Maybe they don't need me.

In fact, in a city full of people desperate to get out, Trisler would have been a good man to have around. That's because he is an expert in transportation planning – his job is to move armies and their supplies.

Trisler has overseen truck transport in Puerto Rico. In Kentucky, he directed the forklifts and cranes that moved cargo onto trains. In 2002, he worked the airfields of Afghanistan.

"Airports, boats, planes, trains and trucks, railroads and buses," Trisler said. "That's what I bring to the table."

On Monday, the levees broke in New Orleans. Water flooded much of the city. The First Army was deployed to Alabama and Mississippi. For Trisler, however, it was a normal day at work.

On Tuesday, "I went to work and came home."

Then his boss called.

Be ready to leave at 5:30 tomorrow morning, she told Trisler. You'll need to update your will, in case anything happens while you're deployed. Then you'll hit the road.

"Great," Trisler said. "I don't want to be on the sidelines for this one."

Trisler drove Lance to baseball practice, his mind racing with the work ahead of him. At the field, he asked the other coaches to cover for him. He'd be back later to get Lance. Then, he drove back to the base to collect his uniform from the dry cleaner, and ran several other errands. Finally, he picked up Lance and drove home to tell Maribel, his wife. After 11 years of marriage, she wasn't surprised.

"Every time that something major happens concerning this country, I know that he has to go," she said. "It's his job."

They left Fort Sam Houston early Wednesday, a team of two dozen men in rented Ford Excursions. "We probably looked like the presidential cavalcade, coming into New Orleans," Trisler said, chuckling. "All of us in uniform, stopping on the way to buy coolers and ice and toilet paper."

The convoy stopped at a gas station about 45 miles from Baton Rouge. Trisler wanted to fill up, just in case there were shortages farther in. He also bought a street map of New Orleans.

"If I show up in New Orleans as the transportation officer without a friggin' map," he said to himself, "I'm gonna look like an idiot."

Darkness had fallen by the time they reached the emergency operations center in Baton Rouge on Wednesday night. After being briefed on conditions inside New Orleans, Trisler and his colleagues got their orders – take charge of the hundreds of buses lined up at a gas station on the outskirts of the city. Move them into New Orleans, and get the people out.

Their mission was a departure from the sort of behind-the-scenes planning Fifth Army officers are accustomed to, said Major Andy Gilbert, who was traveling with Trisler in the same SUV along with another major, David Parker. "It was just a sort of, 'Hey you, we need your help. Go and do this. Help get people on buses,'" Gilbert said.

It was one o'clock early Thursday morning and 80 percent of New Orleans was underwater. Trisler and Gilbert had been told what to expect, but nothing could have prepared them for what they were about to see.

If he had known, Trisler said later, maybe he and his colleagues wouldn't have stopped for coffee before heading to New Orleans. But as it was, they had been up for nearly 24 hours. They had a feeling it would be a long time before they slept again. "We knew that we were just getting started," Trisler said.

So the men stopped at a donut shop just off Interstate 10 and ordered giant cups of coffee. The stop took maybe ten minutes, but it would haunt Trisler in the weeks to come. "That ten-minute hesitation could have been another bus loaded," he said. "It wasn't a mistake, but it's one of those things that you've got to live with from now on."

Trisler, Gilbert and Parker's assignment was to evacuate the intersection of Interstate 10 and Causeway Boulevard in Metairie, a suburb just west of New Orleans. Normally, the spot was a busy interchange between I-10, the main highway linking New Orleans to Baton Rouge, and Causeway Boulevard, which takes motorists across Lake Pontchartrain.

But in the aftermath of Hurricane Katrina, the intersection had been transformed into a makeshift evacuation point, triage center, refugee camp and – increasingly – a hazardous waste site.

As Gilbert pulled their Excursion into the intersection, Trisler saw hundreds – perhaps thousands – of people pressed against concrete barriers that penned them onto a cloverleaf south of the interstate. A row of policemen stood alongside the barriers and as Trisler watched them he sensed their fear. "They were hoping the situation just didn't explode," he said.

"It was just a mass of people," Gilbert said. "I've never seen so many people just packed into a place like that."

As he got out of the truck, Trisler ran the numbers through his head again, the same ones he had been working on since Baton Rouge. We can put 40 people on a bus, he thought. Ten buses can move 400 people. We've got 150 buses. That means we can move 6,000 people. No one had any idea how many people were already on the interstate, but some estimates were in the thousands.

We need to get started, he thought.

Trisler called Major Derrick Ward, who was waiting with the buses outside of the city. We're ready, he said.

By daylight, the buses were moving. But their arrival was erratic. Sometimes, only three would show up, the rest having been diverted elsewhere in the chaos of the evacuation. An hour later, 15 would show up at once. Then, nothing.

Gilbert fielded questions from the evacuees as best he could. "We're trying to get buses here," he remembers telling them. But it was hard to reassure them when he himself didn't know why the buses weren't coming more frequently. "I tried not to be nervous and worry them more, but it was very frustrating to me, not being able to tell them, yeah, there's 100 buses on the way."

Finally, between 8 a.m. and noon, the evacuation picked up. "It really started to flow," Trisler said.

But after dozens of buses had come and gone, he noticed that the crowd didn't seem to be shrinking. Just as quickly as Trisler, Gilbert and Parker could load them onto buses, more people were arriving. Some wandered in on their own. Others were getting rescued from boats, then loaded onto trucks, which dropped them off at the interstate. And every few minutes, helicopters landed on the northeastern cloverleaf – so many that others circled above, waiting their turn.

But Trisler wasn't paying attention. "I'm down here working buses. I'm not realizing that slowly, minute by minute, hour by hour, people are getting dumped on top of us."

With the buses moving steadily, Trisler thought he might have some time to step back and fine-tune the system.

But as he stood there, people began to approach him with their problems.

"You couldn't look at a person who didn't have a problem to tell you about," he said. And every problem, he said, was serious.

But Trisler had only one thing to offer them: A bus.

Dirty diaper?

"Ma'am, all I have is a bus."

Nine stitches?

"Get on the bus. They'll take you to a better place."

Broken leg?

"All I've got is a bus."

Then he met the seven children.

Suddenly, a bus wasn't going to do it.

In Trisler's 18 years in the army, he had been through countless exercises known in training as "scenarios."

Instructors throw out a scenario – a major earthquake, a dirty-bomb explosion, a suicide attack – and participants divide into teams to figure out how to resolve the problem.

One team attacks transportation. Another group handles security. Still others take charge of shelters, media, logistics. As they work these scenarios, sometimes the instructor will walk into the room and throw them what's known as a "measle."

Is the scenario an earthquake? Then guess what – a chemical plant just exploded.

Does the scenario involve a refugee camp? One of the babies has a bomb in its diaper.

By Thursday afternoon, "I had gone through every scenario I'd ever seen or heard or done in my life, plus 200 more that hadn't been written yet," Trisler said. "And then the kids showed up."

The kids were one big measle.

It was just after noon when the woman first walked up to Trisler and asked for his help. By that time, most of those who wanted to leave had already been loaded on buses, headed for Houston and Dallas and who knew where else. Now Trisler, Gilbert and Parker worked the crowd, asking those who remained why they hadn't boarded a bus.

She was a young woman – in her early 30s, perhaps – and had close-cropped hair. She was wearing glasses and a camouflage tank top.

In one arm slept a chubby, doe-eyed baby boy, four months old at most. He wasn't hers, she told Trisler.

In fact, of the eight other children that surrounded her, only two belonged to her. The rest, she said, lived in her apartment building. When the helicopter landed on their roof, the pilot said he was only taking children. The woman – Trisler would later learn her name was Shawn Jackson – had managed to jump on at the last minute.

Trisler could have told the woman what he told the man with the broken arm, or what he told the woman with a dirty diaper: Get on a bus.

But for reasons he can't quite explain, that wasn't an acceptable answer.

One thing he knew: The four-month-old baby wasn't getting on the bus. And if the baby didn't get on the bus, his six-year-old brother – De'Monté was his name – wasn't getting on a bus either.

Then there were the rest of them, all one- and two-year-olds. "If you can't say your name and say your address, you're not going anywhere," Trisler decided.

Together, Trisler and Jackson quizzed De'Monté. The baby was his brother. The two-year-old girl and the one-year-old boy were his cousins. The other kids he didn't know, but he had seen them in the building. His aunt's name was FeFe.

Trisler decided De'Monté knew enough. "As long as they all stayed together, they could piece it all together and find one of the parents to identify all the rest of them," he reasoned.

After calling his commanders in Baton Rouge, Trisler learned that the state Department of Social Services was in charge of children who had become separated from their parents. They had even set up a special children-only shelter in Baton Rouge. Wait there, he was told. DSS is on its way.

Trisler returned to the buses. A part of him didn't mind waiting for DSS. If we wait long enough, he thought, maybe the parents will show up on one of these helicopters.

An hour passed, and Jackson approached him again. "Just to have yourself in that situation was enough of a struggle. You can't imagine that woman having the seven kids," Trisler said. "She was about ten steps away from a bus going to San Antonio."

And yet, because of the kids, she couldn't get on.

Finally, Trisler walked back to the triage area and spoke to some medical workers. The children, he figured, could be considered "special needs" people – a category the medical workers were responsible for. Eventually, they worked out a plan – a group of state mental health workers would care for the kids until DSS arrived to drive them to Baton Rouge. Shawn Jackson was free to go.

Trisler picked up two-year-old Gabrielle, who was sleeping on a chair. He slung her over one shoulder and reached out his hand to Dejahney. She started to cry. He picked her up anyway.

As he hoisted Dejahney onto his hip, anger overwhelmed him.

"I kept thinking it would resolve itself," he said. But as he held the two girls in his arms, he thought to himself, "You just bought this. You've got to truly live with this for the rest of your life."

As he walked toward the medical tent, he turned his head one more time toward the helicopters. At that moment, a photographer snapped his picture. "I was just kind of pissed off and mad," he said. "I was like, you'd better bring the fucking parents. Just bring the friggin' parents now."

The anger, he said, was only a way to keep other emotions at bay. "I knew that when I pulled them away from that last link to their parents (Shawn Jackson), that we were doing something very crucial. That we were now going to leave all ties with a four-month-old and a couple of two-year-olds and some kids that don't know their names or addresses," he said. "The only thing we've got right now at that point in time was De'Monté."

Walking behind Trisler was Russell Semon, a counselor and administrator for the state Office of Mental Health. In his arms was Leewood, who seemed lethargic and non-responsive. When they reached the medical area, Semon laid him down on a cot and called over a paramedic. Leewood was fine, they decided. He was probably just exhausted.

Trisler set Dejahney and Gabrielle on a stretcher. As he laid them down, he spoke softly. "You guys are gonna ride in an ambulance and you might get to take an airplane," he told them. "We'll find your mom and dad."

One of the girls – he can't remember which – just stared back at him. "She just kind of laid down, like I was going to change her diaper," he said. "She had that diaper-change look in her eyes. And I just smiled at her so she didn't start crying."

Trisler glanced at De'Monté and the other children and walked back toward the buses.

Once Trisler left, most of the kids fell asleep. Everyone, that is, except De'Monte and Zarione. After scarfing down cookies and strawberry Pop-Tarts, the two found a wheelchair that wasn't being used and began giving each other rides.

Semon and his colleagues had only been on I-10 for a few hours when they were assigned the seven children. As mental health workers, their assignment was to mingle with the crowd and identify people who needed help. "We were trying to deal with the tragedy and the anxiety with having just been in New Orleans," he said. "We were listening to what they had to say and trying to identify those who might need a higher level of intervention."

But once the children arrived, the rest of their work went by the wayside. De'Monté, in particular, was a handful. Fueled by the strawberry Pop-Tarts or perhaps by anxiety, De'Monté darted in and out of the cots and zipped onto the street.

"What's wrong with him?" the National Guardsmen would ask as they herded him back toward the medical area.

At one point, Dr. Jody Meek, a psychiatrist for the state Office of Mental Health, wondered if De'Monté was hyperactive. "He wouldn't sit still," he said. Even when Semon lifted him onto his hip, "he was yelling at the top of his lungs, and taking his cap and throwing it on the ground," Meeks said. "He was very difficult."

Zarione wouldn't stop exploring.

By that time, I-10 was a dirty, dangerous place. IV bags and needles crunched underfoot, Meek said. It had rained earlier in the day, and now food and mud mixed together to create a sticky, smelly mess. He was horrified when Zarione found a pair of shoes lying on the ground and put them on her feet.

Hours passed, and DSS was nowhere to be found. At one point, Semon said, they almost sent the kids to Baton Rouge with a pair of television reporters. But the journalists backed out.

Trisler checked back a few times. Every time he discovered the children still had not left, his frustration grew. By late afternoon, he had said goodbye to De'Monte several times, each time thinking it would be his last.

"I wanted closure with him and I wanted to say goodbye to him," he said.

Finally, around dusk, Trisler checked back one more time. The children were gone. An ambulance had taken them to Baton Rouge.

"About damn time," Trisler said.

Chapter Six
A PROMISE BROKEN

Twenty-five minutes.

Catrina and Felecia huddled under their father's umbrella as they willed the minutes to pass.

In less than half an hour, they'd be on dry land, safely reunited with their babies.

Despite the rain, the women refused to head for the shelter of their apartments. "We are not about to get off this roof," Catrina remembers deciding, "because we want to get rescued to be with our kids."

Plenty of helicopters circled overhead, but none seemed bound for 3223 Third Street. Hueys, Chinooks and Dolphin vessels passed above, and their colors ranged from the orange-and-white of the Coast Guard choppers to the green of the Army helicopters. Paul Riley kept an eye out for the small, dark-green helicopter that had rescued the children.

"Every time we'd see a helicopter, we'd be like, 'That's it, that's it," Keyshawn said.

But Paul's answer was always the same: "That ain't it."

Twenty-five minutes came and went, and still they waited.

Five hours passed. The rain stopped, and it got hot again.

Finally, Paul spotted a dark-green helicopter. He flagged it down.

"Where are the kids?" Felecia asked when the helicopter landed.

The pilot had no idea what she was talking about.

"Just get on," she remembers him saying. "We're gonna bring you there."

The pilot's message unsettled the women, but they felt they had no choice. It was early evening. The pilot who had rescued the children clearly wasn't coming back.

As they approached the helicopter, the wind from its blades nearly blew the women off their feet. Felecia felt thankful for the heavy book bag she carried on her back as she crawled toward the helicopter on her knees.

Because there was no room for the men, the women said goodbye to Darryl, Adrian, Paul and the others. Yowanda's boyfriend, Leewood Moore, convinced the pilot to let him on because she was diabetic.

As the helicopter rose, the mothers gazed down on their ruined city.

"Tears wanted to come but we tried to hold it in," Keyshawn said. She saw water licking at the eaves of houses, and gaping holes in the sides of buildings. She recoiled in shock when she saw the battered roof of the Superdome, then felt relieved the family had decided not to spend the hurricane there.

Keyshawn's mother, Patricia, couldn't stop her tears. They curled under her chin as she flew through the air. "I'm looking at houses underwater and I'm like, this is my life," she said. "This is my life here. And just like that, it's gone."

Less than 15 minutes later, the women landed at Lakefront Airport, a general aviation airport in eastern New Orleans.

Lakefront was hardly an ideal spot for an evacuation. As its name implies, the airport borders Lake Pontchartrain. Its runway juts right into the water, a man-made peninsula that sits eight feet above sea level.

On Monday, the storm surge from Hurricane Katrina obliterated the first floor of the airport's main administration building and scattered the airplanes like plastic toys. No levee stands between the lake and the airport, a fact that both exposed Lakefront to the full brunt of the storm but also allowed it to quickly recover. Unlike parts of town where the levees prevented the water from receding back into the lake, the water at the airport subsided.

On Tuesday – two days before the mothers' arrival – airport director Randolph Taylor was assessing the hurricane's damage in his Dodge Durango pickup truck when he spotted an orange-and-white Coast Guard helicopter coming his way.

With the runway still underwater and debris everywhere, the helicopter's arrival was a surprise, to say the least.

Taylor's air-to-ground radio squawked: "Lakefront Tower."

"Lakefront Tower is down," Taylor answered. "What are your intentions?"

"I'm landing on the street," the pilot said. "This has been designated an evacuation drop-off and pickup point."

The news surprised Taylor, but he took it in stride. Within minutes, he went from being an airport director to the head of a hurricane evacuation center.

By Wednesday, the helicopters were arriving in swarms. By then, the waters receded from the runways and they became the center of the operation. Because the airport was surrounded by water in all directions – Lake Pontchartrain to the north and the flooded city to the west, south and east – the only way out was by air. So after the Coast Guard rescued the victims from the rooftops, the evacuees had to wait on the runway for a ride on an Army helicopter somewhere else.

The Coast Guard helicopters worked around the clock. Sometimes Taylor counted as many as a dozen choppers on the runway at once, with some unloading and others picking up.

Taylor and his men – a handful of airport workers, firefighters, and later about 10 state police officers – had the task of maintaining order and keeping thousands of people fed and as comfortable as possible.

Because he was so short-staffed, he enlisted the help of able-bodied evacuees to unload the military meals and water that the Coast Guard dropped on the runways. Taylor and his men found a handful of portable toilets, scrubbed them down, and put them to use. The only shelter from the sweltering heat was three fire trucks and the employees' own cars, including Taylor's Durango and another man's Jeep.

When the elderly or the sick arrived, "We'd just put them inside and let them sit there. To get out of the sun," Taylor said.

Helicopters weren't the only ones bringing in evacuees. As one of the few areas of high ground in east New Orleans – one of the most devastated neighborhoods in the city – Lakefront quickly became a point of convergence.

Taylor would see them arriving along the normally scenic Lakeshore Drive – pushing the sick in shopping carts and carrying their belongings in plastic garbage bags. Anything with wheels was pressed into service. "They were bringing people in front-end loaders," he said. Everyone got on the helicopters. "We loaded them up and sent them on their way."

Despite the throngs of helicopters, the wait for an Army chopper lasted several hours, Taylor said. On Thursday night – when Catrina, Felecia and the mothers touched down – the airport had about 500 evacuees waiting for a helicopter. By Friday morning, he said, the number grew to about 2,000 people.

Catrina started running as soon as her feet touched land. "I was expecting to see my kids," she said. "I'm like okay, we about to go get our kids."

Like the I-10 and Causeway intersection, trash and discarded water bottles littered the runway and an open field where most of the people were gathered. The smell of sweat and human waste hung thick in the air.

But what Catrina noticed were the children. "I saw a lot of people with their kids," she said. "And I asked myself, 'Why the hell have they got their kids and I don't have mine?'"

She approached a police officer, who was standing with some men wearing military fatigues.

"Have you seen my kids?" she asked. "There's like about seven kids. They don't have no parents and we're looking for them. I have two sons, and I've got a niece and a nephew."

The answer made Catrina's blood run hot.

"Ma'am," they answered. "Any kids are with their parents."

That did it. "We went to going off," Catrina said.

Someone sobbed. Someone else cursed.

Catrina remembers that Yowanda started shouting. "How could they do that? How could they separate the parents from the kids? These people don't know our kids," she yelled.

"I have a four-month-old baby," Catrina added.

But the men had nothing to tell them. They didn't know anything about their kids. And they had never heard of Overleaf, Texas.

Over the next few hours, the women went from police officers to National Guardsmen to firefighters and even reporters.

Some people, they learned, were being sent to Dallas. Others were headed for Houston. Still others were being evacuated to San Antonio. But no one had heard about the children. And no one had heard of Overleaf, Texas.

Then, at some point in the night, there was a flash of hope. One of the women who lived in their apartment building – and had left in the same helicopter – heard De'Monté's name on the radio.

"Catrina Williams?" the woman asked.

"Yeah, that's me," she answered.

"Do you have a son named De'Monté Love?"

"Yeah."

"Well, he's looking for you." She said. "The people say to get in touch with the state police. And the state police are going to give you information."

Catrina frantically searched for a state policeman.

Finally, she found one.

"Did y'all hear of a De'Monté Love asking for Catrina Williams?" she asked him.

Their answer again deflated her.

"Ma'am we didn't hear anything."

"But this lady just came and told me my son is asking for me," she pleaded. "He's separated from me and I'm trying to contact him."

The man just shook his head, she said. "There's no way we could possibly give you that information," he said. "The only thing we can tell you is that y'all are leaving tomorrow. Ya'll going to be going to one part of Texas. That's where your kids should be at."

Disheartened, Catrina, Felecia and the other mothers stood in the line – which was already hundreds deep – bound for the Louis Armstrong International Airport and eventually a plane to Texas.

But as night fell, the helicopters stopped flying out. The women ate some of the military meals that rescue workers were handing out, and looked for a place to sleep.

Eventually, Marcie and the others commandeered some boxes of water bottles, turning them on their side so they could sleep on cardboard rather than the filthy field.

It was hot, and the hordes of people nearby made it feel even hotter.

"People were laying on the ground – I mean, old people who can't lay on the ground," Marcie said.

With the power still out, the field was dark, save for the flashing lights of a few fire trucks.

"We were going to have to sleep without our kids," Marcie said.

This wasn't the way it was supposed to have happened.

Chapter Seven
THE ROAD TO BATON ROUGE

Like Noah and his ark, Pat Coveney brought two of everything.

In the Ford F-150 pickup that Coveney drove, he had packed two alternators, two water pumps, two radiators, and two tire jacks. Not to mention tires, oil, oil filters, light bulbs, stretchers, and extra oxygen.

All of it was for the two ambulances that on Wednesday night, August 31, sped east on Interstate 10 from Houston.

Coveney and the eight paramedics he brought with him had no idea what they would find once they got to New Orleans. But in the world of emergency medical services, said Raymond Massie, one of Coveney's paramedics, "we're trained to plan for the worst and hope for the best."

In its four years in business, Coveney's company, Allyn Medical Services, had been doing well as a private ambulance outfit. In addition to the run-of-the-mill assignments – providing support for charity bike rides, rodeos and high school football games – Allyn Medical had also developed a niche as a transporter of premature and newborn babies.

The two ambulances that now raced toward Louisiana were outfitted with incubators and portable ventilators, special equipment that put Allyn Medical near the top of the Texas Department of Health's priority list when it came to natural disasters. Coveney had gotten the call earlier Wednesday evening.

After packing his truck and the ambulances with every possible supply, Coveney and his men gassed up and headed out of Houston. Cities flashed past in the humid night – Beaumont, Lake Charles, Lafayette, and finally Baton Rouge, the ambulances' first stop.

It was 4 a.m. on Thursday morning when Coveney and his men pulled into a parking lot at Jimmy Swaggart Ministries, where the Louisiana Department of Health and Hospitals had set up its emergency operations center and ambulance staging area.

The headquarters of the televangelist's spiritual empire is a rambling 200-acre campus off Bluebonnet Boulevard in Baton Rouge, not too far from the giant Mall of Louisiana. After more than a decade of decline following a highly publicized sex scandal and feuds with other televangelists, several of Swaggart's buildings now lie empty or are leased to state agencies.

Despite the hour, the parking lot was packed. When he checked in with the command center, Coveney learned that Allyn Medical was the 143rd ambulance service to report for duty. In addition to Louisiana and Texas, Coveney spotted ambulances from Kentucky, South Carolina, even Pennsylvania. By the end of the week, all 48 of the continental states were represented in the Jimmy Swaggart parking lot.

"You name it, they were there," Coveney said.

Before long, the men got their first assignment. Take your ambulances to the intersection of I-10 and Causeway Boulevard. Load up with patients, and carry them back to Baton Rouge. Repeat.

The command center officials had briefed the men on what conditions were like, but Coveney and his workers were still surprised when they pulled into the intersection early Thursday morning. About 100 ambulances were already on scene, lining up behind the triage area like the taxi line in front of Manhattan's Grand Central Station.

"At that point I was in awe," said Brian Sizemore, who normally supervises Allyn's neo-natal team at Texas Children's Hospital. On this trip, he was a medic and one of the ambulance drivers. "I could not believe the amount of people, the amount of chaos, that was going on. We just did not know that it was going to be like that. I mean, nobody did."

From a medical viewpoint, many of the evacuees' problems were minor – what paramedics call the "walking wounded." Because so many had been stranded for days on rooftops with little water, dehydration was the main ailment the men encountered. Coveney could pick out the dehydration victims as they walked toward him.

"They had the sunken eyes, the skin wrinkled up, barely can walk," he said. "They were begging for water."

Most patients were those with chronic conditions – diabetics, kidney patients – who had gone for days without medication or dialysis. They would be fine if Massie, Sizemore and Coveney could get them to a hospital in time.

Once they arrived at the I-10 intersection, the system was relatively simple. Coveney and the others would park their ambulances and let the on-scene commander know they were available. Then, when their turn came, they'd fill the ambulance with patients and take them to one of several treatment centers in Baton Rouge.

"We'd haul butt," Massie said. Seventy to eighty miles an hour was the norm, he said.

Coveney's ambulances shuttled back and forth all day Thursday. Sometimes they would drop the patients at a makeshift hospital that had been set up at the Louisiana State University campus. Other times they'd take them to Baton Rouge General Hospital.

Then, late in the afternoon, Coveney stopped in at the I-10 command area to pass along some good news – he had spotted a few gas stations along the route that were being kept open for emergency vehicles.

As he was standing there, a woman from the Louisiana Department of Health and Hospitals came up to him. She was looking for seven different trucks to transport seven children who had been separated from their parents, she said.

Why get seven different trucks when they'd fit in one ambulance? Coveney asked.

"Put them in my truck," he said. "We'll take them."

Coveney pulled aside Massie and Sizemore, two men that Coveney knew he could trust. Both had young children of their own, and Sizemore worked with kids all the time at Texas Children's Hospital.

"I've got a special assignment for you," Coveney told the men. Both agreed to take the job.

Coveney copied down their driver's license numbers. He wrote down the phone number of the woman in the health department, as well as those they would be meeting in Baton Rouge. He didn't want to take any chances.

Sizemore pulled the ambulance into the triage area.

Some of the children were sleeping. A paramedic from another ambulance company was holding the baby, who was asleep in his arms.

"I just fell in love with them, right then and there," Sizemore said. "I vowed at that point to take care of them."

The children were dirty, tired and – with the exception of De'Monté – unusually quiet.

"To be honest with you, I think all those kids were in shock," Coveney said.

Coveney could tell the children came from good homes. The baby, he said, was a little chubby. "Not late for dinner," Coveney joked.

One of the girls – she would later turn out to be Zarione – wore earrings. The others wore neatly braided hair and nice-quality clothes. Coveney thought it was likely that they came from a middle-class family.

"That was very, very obvious just by what they had on and the jewelry they were wearing," he said.

De'Monté didn't want to get into the ambulance. Coveney coaxed him with drinks. 'We've got Cokes, we've got water," he told De'Monté.

Enticed by a bottle of green Gatorade, De'Monté finally got in.

While Semon and Meeks – the mental health workers who had been caring for the kids – watched, Coveney, Massie and Sizemore made sure the children were comfortable in the ambulance. They lay the baby and one of the smaller toddlers on the ambulance's stretcher, then strapped them in. They placed the other children in seats, rolling up towels and sheets to make sure the seatbelts fit snugly over their laps.

Because the back of the ambulance was cold, they tucked towels around the kids' shoulders.

As they worked, they wondered what had happened to the children's parents. Much of the information Shawn Jackson and De'Monté had given Major Steven Trisler had already been lost in the chaos of the day.

"My mind was going 90 miles a minute to figure out what was going on," Sizemore said. "I just couldn't understand why these children were by themselves to begin with. And you know, where did they come from?"

Massie spoke softly to the children, aware that all the new faces must have been scary. "I told them what my name was and that we were going to take really good care of them, not to worry, and that we would reunite them with our families as quickly as possible," he said.

Sizemore wrapped a towel around Dejahney and asked her if she was all right.

"And she just looked at me. Just dazed," he said. "I don't know if she understood what I was talking about at all."

Once everyone was warm and strapped into their seatbelts, Coveney shut the ambulance doors.

Where are the parents? He asked himself. Did they leave the kids in order to save themselves? Or were the parents dead, and would these children now have to live with that for the rest of their lives? In his 18 years as a paramedic, "I've seen a lot of deaths with infants and kids, being on the streets and things like that. But you know, you see these kids sitting there with no parents, it really tends to bother you."

As Sizemore prepared to pull away, he said, Coveney laid down the rules.

"You do not speed. You go the speed limit. And you watch every turn."

Along the way, Sizemore tried to get information from De'Monté. "But he clammed up every time," he said. "He would say something, but it wasn't anything I could understand."

Like any children on a long car ride, the kids fell asleep and the rest of the trip was uneventful.

Department of Health workers were waiting for the ambulance when it pulled into Jimmy Swaggart Ministries an hour and a half later.

Coveney, Massie and Sizemore unloaded the children and, with the help of medics at the scene, took the children inside to the emergency operations center, where a doctor would examine them.

Sizemore gathered up Dejahney and brought her inside. As they waited for a doctor, he cradled Dejahney in his arms. She fiddled with his pen, rubbed the stubble on his cheek, and then lay her head on his shoulder. "She basically felt loved at that point," he said.

As much as they wanted to stay, plenty more patients needed their help. Massie and Coveney prepared to leave.

But when Sizemore went to give Dejahney to someone else, she screamed.

Dejahney had found someone to love her for the first time since being separated from her mother eight hours earlier.

She wasn't about to let go.

Chapter Eight
LEAVING LOUISIANA

The morning sun did nothing to freshen the hot, putrid air that hung over Lakefront Airport on Friday, September 2.

Atop the boxes of water bottles, the mothers stirred.

Sleep had been fitful, at best. Although the Army helicopters had stopped taking people from the airport, the Coast Guard helicopters worked through the night, rescuing people from their roofs. And a bed of boxes isn't exactly comfortable.

By morning, the crowd had grown from hundreds to over a thousand people.

Catrina and the others left their makeshift beds and ate a breakfast of military meals and water. "Then the sun came out and everybody started getting disgusted again," she said. "The heat, I mean, the heat! Oh, Lord."

Around this time, the Army helicopters began flying again and the mothers got in line. The night before, the women had been only tenth in line to get on a helicopter. Now, with the arrival of so many new people, "we went all the way to the back of the line," Catrina said.

Although most of the Army helicopters were large Chinooks, which hold 30 people or more, the helicopter that the women boarded was the same size that had taken them from their roofs – a small, dark-green helicopter that only held their group.

Maj. Steven Trisler holding Gabrielle Alexander, asleep on his right shoulder, and Zarione Love.

Brent Broussard and Dejahncy sit in the hallway outside the children's shelter in Baton Rouge.

The Big Buddy volunteers. Top row, left to right. Unknown, Derrick Robertson, Brent Broussard, Dejahney, Zarione, Jodi McKenzie, Lauren Billon, Leewood. Second row, left to right: Ty're, Ura Gold, Ina Perkins, Da'Roneal, Kori Thomas, Gabby, De'Monté, Ursula Gold.

Tyre climbs onto his bed in the children's shelter in Baton Rouge.

Marceline Alexander anxiously awaiting the reunion with her daughter, Gabrielle.

Marceline Alexander reunited with her daughter, Gabrielle.

Felecia Love reunited with Da'Roneal.

Catrina Williams waits for a taxi outside the KellyUSA shelter in San Antonio with her son, Da'Roneal.

Da'Roneal Williams in his stroller.

De'Monté Love sits on his bed in the family's hotel room in San Antonio.

Marceline Alexander fixes the hair of her daughter, Gabrielle, in their new apartment in Dallas.

The sisters get their nails done near their hotel in San Antonio. Left to right, Felecia Love, Catrina Williams, their sister Alisha Nelson, and her daughters, Gerall'ycia and Ja'Monica.

Felecia's son Ty're smiles while waiting for his mom to get her nails done.

De'Monté mugs for the camera in his hotel room.

The women weren't sure where they were headed. Catrina thought they might be flying to Texas – Overleaf, she hoped. Once again, Patricia Carter looked down on her flooded city. This time she wondered about her son and her other daughter, from whom she hadn't heard since the storm began.

"I was just watching the water, wondering if my children was one of the bodies that was floating around in that water," she said.

The helicopter touched down several minutes later at Louis Armstrong International Airport in Kenner, 19 miles west of Lakefront.

As they climbed off the helicopter, the scene looked familiar.

Hordes of people squatted on curbs or sat on the sidewalks, sweating under a blistering heat. Trash covered the pavement outside of the airport terminals. The smell of human sweat and filth was everywhere. Without any electricity or air conditioning, the inside of the airport was no better.

Despite the miserable landscape, the mothers couldn't have arrived at a better time. On Friday, more than a dozen airlines and cargo operators began flying citizens out of the city for the first time since the hurricane had hit four days earlier.

With helicopters arriving every few minutes, the airplanes couldn't keep up with the demand. Long lines snaked through concourses, with airport workers shouting out the number of empty seats.

But the mothers ignored the lines, heading instead for the first official people they could find. Within minutes, any hope of finding their children again evaporated. Their questions were met only with apologies and shakes of the head. Mentions of Overleaf, Texas got a blank stare.

At one point, Catrina found a man who seemed to be in charge. But all the man knew was where the food line was.

Facing a second day without their children, the mothers' tempers rose.

"It was a lot of people saying 'Calm down, calm down," Keyshawn said. "And we were upset. Fussing. This is our kids. Y'all can't tell us to calm down."

Catrina started feeling dizzy. She couldn't breathe. She was suffering from a panic attack.

Someone, she doesn't know who, carried her to the medical triage area. In addition to being an evacuation point, since Thursday night government officials had designated the airport as a temporary field hospital. If the scene in the concourses was miserable, the view inside the field hospital was straight out of hell.

Officials had planned for the arrival of hundreds of patients, but when thousands showed up, they couldn't keep up. Patients lay on stretchers not far from ticket counters and baggage carousels, and so many were dying that the airport set up a morgue.

"Oh, my God, it's overwhelming. Hundreds of people. Everybody needs something, and you don't know where to start," volunteer nurse Nanette Nealy told the Washington Post.

When Catrina looked at the swarm of the sick and dying around her, she knew she didn't belong. "I ain't never going to get out of here," she said to herself.

Meanwhile, back in the concourses, there was a spark of good news.

The mothers, it turned out, weren't the only ones to know the name De'Monté Love. Somewhere in the throng, Major Steven Trisler was directing buses, helping school buses and coaches navigate between the Superdome, other evacuation points and the airport. Russell Semon and Dr. Jody Meek – the mental health workers – were there, too, helping out in the triage area.

While Meek mingled among the sick, assessing who needed medication or psychological counseling, a National Guard soldier approached him. What was the plan for children, he asked. He had a woman who was responsible for several kids, he said, and she didn't want to take care of them in another state.

Meek cringed. "We would take them, but we were crippled yesterday because we were babysitting these kids," he told the soldier, recounting the story of the seven children that he and Semon had babysat on I-10. "Surely FEMA has some plan."

The soldier nodded and disappeared.

Meanwhile, Marcie and Yowanda, who had separated themselves from the others, were waiting in line for a plane to San Antonio.

But as Marcie sat there, something told her not to give up. "Something told me just to ask, just to be serious about it," she said.

So she stepped out of line and asked a National Guard soldier for help.

"Well," the soldier told her, "I have somebody you could talk to about this."

A few minutes later, the soldier was leading Marcie toward Meek.

"I put my kids on a helicopter. We thought the helicopter was coming back and it didn't," Marcie told him.

"Ma'am, what are the kids names?" Meek asked.

Marcie went through the list of those whose names she could remember.

"Were there four boys?" Marcie remembers him asking.

"Yes," Marcie said.

"Was the oldest named De'Monté?"

Marcie began to cry.

"I just couldn't believe it," Meek said. Since Thursday, Meek and Semon had been so busy they hadn't had a chance to talk to anyone else about the children. Now, Marcie happened to run into the same National Guard soldier that Meek had just been talking to. "I do feel that God's hand was somehow involved there."

Meek gave Marcie a hug. "Those are your kids, and they are safe," he said. "They're in Baton Rouge."

But despite the good news, there was little hope for a reunification. At that point, government officials were in full-blown crisis mode. Hundreds of people were still stranded on rooftops. The convention center still housed 20,000 increasingly desperate people. The aim was to empty the city of its people, and worry about reuniting families later.

You'll have to get on a plane, Meek told Marcie, and get your kids later.

Marcie ran to tell Catrina, Felecia and the others the news.

Meanwhile, Catrina was still lying in the hospital ward, increasingly horrified at what she saw around her. Old people and others far sicker than herself were crying and begging for medicine. Some were sitting up, but others were too weak to do anything but lie on their stretcher. Catrina knew that her symptoms from the panic attack were nothing compared to the patients that surrounded her.

"I better strengthen my own self up," she said to herself. "I've gotta get up."

Catrina forced herself to sit and drink as much water as she could. She teetered out of the hospital wing and searched for the rest of the mothers.

When Marcie delivered the news, Catrina wanted to hear it from the source.

But by the time they returned to the spot where Meek had been, he was gone. A woman was there instead, and she knew nothing about the children.

The women were back to square one.

Sure, they had learned that the kids were safe in Baton Rouge. But as the hours passed in the chaotic airport, they wondered whether to trust the good news. After all, a helicopter pilot had once told them he would take their children to Overleaf, Texas – a place that didn't even seem to exist. He had told them he would come back for them, only to never return. Now, 24 hours had passed and they still hadn't found their children.

So why should they believe Marcie's news?

And the mothers had other worries, as well. Catrina, in particular, tried not to think about what had happened to her father and her husband.

"I had to put my pain of me missing my husband and my daddy, being worried, wondering if they were being rescued or not, to the side to worry about my kids," Catrina said. "Once I worry about my kids, then I can worry about the next thing."

The reunification came by chance. Yowanda ran into a friend from the neighborhood, who told her that she had seen several men from 3223 Third Street standing in line for airline tickets. The men, it turned out, had waited all night for the next helicopter. Then, earlier that morning, one finally came. Instead of ferrying them to Lakefront Airport, it took them directly to the international airport.

Now, the group had a choice to make. Should they get in line for a bus that would take them to Houston, or fly to San Antonio, which was farther away? Finally – after first standing in a long line for Houston – they decided flying would get them to a shelter more quickly. Once settled there, they could begin the search for their children in earnest.

With the exception of Patricia Carter, who had flown when she was too little to remember it, the flight to San Antonio was the group's first time on an airplane.

"I promised myself in my heart that I wasn't gonna never fly," Catrina said. Air travel just didn't seem natural to her. "As a little kid, I was like, how could they be in that sky? I wasn't gonna never fly."

As the flight attendants explained how to fasten the seatbelts and use the oxygen masks, the women shoved their fear to the side.

"I didn't have no room in my mind to even think about 'Okay, I'm going up in the air.'" Patricia said. "My mind was already full and clouded with all kinds of thoughts. I don't know what it felt like. I really don't know."

Felecia tried to focus on the news that the children were safe in Baton Rouge. "I strongly felt they weren't still in New Orleans," she said. "I'm not saying I knew they were safe. I just had this strong feeling, you know. That they were okay. So I didn't even worry."

The plane taxied along the runway, and the women realized there was no going back. They were leaving their state – and their children – behind.

Keyshawn ached for Dejahney. "I wanted her with me, but then again they said that when we get there, they're gonna find our children," she said.

The jet shot into the sky, pinning Keyshawn to her seat. "As long as we get there and they help us find our children," she thought, "I'll be all right."

Chapter Nine
THE CHILD HEALERS

Brian Sizemore debated what to do.

For nearly a half an hour, little Dejahney had clung to his side at the Department of Health command center in Baton Rouge, unwilling to release her grasp on the first wisp of stability she had found since her mother handed her to Paul Riley several hours earlier.

Now the sun was low in the sky.

In New Orleans, uncounted throngs of the sick and stranded prayed for deliverance from their flooded city. "We had work to do," Sizemore said.

But each time he tried to hand Dejahney to someone else, she screamed.

"She was just clinched onto him," recalled Sizemore's boss, Pat Coveney.

Sizemore glanced at the other children. After the nap on the ambulance, most of the kids were now running around the room. "Everyone fell in love with them," Sizemore said.

Sizemore was happy to see that De'Monté – who was timid in the ambulance – had returned to his boisterous self.

"Obviously he found a place where he was comfortable," Sizemore said. "It was reassuring that he was in a little bit of a better setting and happy with where he was at."

Sizemore sat Dejahney down in a chair and then settled in beside her. Someone had brought in crayons and paper. "I started drawing some stuff with her," he said. "I drew her attention away from me as much as I could."

Then, ever so quietly, Sizemore stood up and tiptoed away. As he left the room, he heard her scream. He kept on walking.

The room where Sizemore, Massie and Coveney brought the children was an unremarkable conference room in the health department's offices at Jimmy Swaggart Ministries. A flat-screen television – connected to the state's videoconferencing system – hung on the wall, its screen dark. Plates of food lay on the table, mingling with crayons and paper for coloring.

By the time the children arrived in Baton Rouge, the information Trisler had tried so hard to collect from De'Monté had been long forgotten. No one had heard of 3223 Third Street, or the story of the helicopter and the pilot who was only taking children.

Once again, De'Monté – a child who had started first grade only a few days earlier and was still learning his ABCs – served as the children's spokesman.

And once again, Catrina's hard work drilling De'Monté on his vital statistics paid off. His mother's name was Catrina Williams, he told the workers. He lived on Third Street in New Orleans. He went to the John W. Hoffman Elementary School. The baby was his brother. Two others were his cousins. The rest of the kids lived in his building.

As De'Monté talked, he nibbled on stalks of raw broccoli that someone had set in front of him.

"What kind of kid is this?" remarked Sharon Howard, the assistant secretary of public health for the state Department of Health and Hospitals, as she watched the six-year-old field questions from health workers, all the while eating his vegetables. "This kid was fabulous."

As the workers watched, they wondered how these children could possibly have gotten separated from their parents. Sure, the hurricane had wreaked havoc on the city – on television, there were reports of looters shooting at helicopters, and people said babies were getting raped at the Superdome. But how could seven children – kids with new sneakers and neatly braided hair and pierced ears – get lost in the crowd? And what kind of mother would give her four-month-old baby to strangers?

On her way to a meeting, Howard noticed a high-level administrator standing by herself in the hallway. She was crying. "She's the kind of person I don't think I've ever seen cry," Howard said.

And she wasn't just sniffling. "I mean, she was hard-down sobbing," Howard said. "She thought someone had actually left these children."

Howard didn't know what had happened to the parents, but she was pretty sure the children hadn't been abandoned. Someone had taught De'Monté to memorize his address, his elementary school, his parents' first and last names. He ate broccoli, for crying out loud. And the baby, Da'Roneal, didn't look like he skipped many meals. "You can tell if children have been raised in a certain way," Howard said.

During one of the twice-daily conference calls with health department administrators throughout the state, Howard mentioned the seven children they had in their custody, and how the kids had been separated from their parents.

Listening in from a special-needs shelter in Thibodeaux, Louisiana, was Dr. Takeisha Davis, a regional medical director for the state Office of Public Health. Howard's words send a shiver of excitement through her spine. Seven kids? Could that possibly be right?

Two days ago, a woman had climbed off a bus from New Orleans and raced into the Thibodeaux shelter, expecting to be reunited her seven children. She and her kids had been rescued from their flooded home and taken to a staging area much like the Interstate 10 intersection. Because of the short supply of buses, the drivers were only taking children and the elderly. We're are all going to the same place, the driver told the woman. You'll be reunited with your children once we get there.

For two days, the mother had been inconsolable. Davis and a social worker had been calling every shelter in the state, without any leads on the seven small children. Now, Howard's words rang in her ears. Davis spoke up.

"Seven children?" she asked. "We have a mother here at the shelter who has *lost* seven children."

"Oh Lord, we got a match," Howard exclaimed.

Howard and Davis' social worker agreed to call each other once the conference call was over. As she waited, Howard delivered the promising news to those who were caring for the children. "We all got excited," Howard said.

Minutes later, Howard got on the phone with the Thibodeaux social worker. But as the woman told the mother's story, Howard's hopes drooped. Incredibly, it was the wrong group of seven children.

The women hung up the phone.

"I guess it just a left a pit in all of our stomachs because we began to realize that this was much larger than we thought," Davis said.

For days, Howard had been hearing about the chaos in the city. "But when I saw those seven kids back there and it was the wrong seven," Howard said, "that's when it clearly became evident to me that this was a widespread problem."

As the children darted about or scribbled with crayons, the conference room slowly filled. Someone cradled the baby in her arms. Others held the toddlers, or played peek-a-boo and hide-and-seek.

"From the highest level person to clerical people, everyone got involved," Howard said. Something about the kids' ability to laugh and play in the midst of calamity was intoxicating, and the workers drank the children's innocence like an elixir. "You were looking for something that you could get some gratification from…people needed to be doing something that they felt was successful," Howard said.

Dr. Erin Brewer wasn't looking for that kind of gratification when she made her way toward the children that Thursday night, but she ended up finding it anyway.

As medical director for the Office of Public Health, Brewer had been working since before the hurricane to set up special-needs shelters for the sick and chronically ill, then to help run the health departments' emergency operations center.

"We had spent the week sending ambulances in and having them be turned away. We were just so upset and frustrated and feeling really, honestly, helpless. I mean, just disappointed in the situation," Brewer said. For reasons no one could explain, she said, health officials kept sending ambulances into New Orleans, only to have them be turned back by the National Guard, state police, and other agencies. Sometimes – especially if one of the emergency vehicles was unmarked – the drivers not only had to have proper identification, they also had to have documentation that they had a specific assignment that required them to enter. "Disappointed didn't even start to explain it," Brewer said.

Then a health worker walked up to her. Would she mind examining some children that some EMS workers had brought in? They were separated from their parents, and now they were here, waiting for the Department of Social Services to pick them up.

The children lured her in.

With the exception of Dejahney, who wasn't taking the departure of Brian Sizemore well, the rest of the children had happily settled into their new reality. De'Monté still sat at a table, politely answering questions.

"He would eat a few bites, and then he would talk," Brewer recalled.

Brewer was exhausted and frustrated, but these children – these "little resilient people" – had been through so much more and had come through relatively unscathed. The children needed food and drink and a snuggle – needs that could be easily met. In New Orleans, scores of patients and elderly people were fighting death as they waited in hospitals and nursing homes for the ambulances and helicopters that Brewer couldn't get to them. But the children, Dr. Brewer said, "they just needed to be taken care of like children do."

After she looked every child over and declared each in good health, she surveyed the room again.

One of the boys – he wouldn't say his name, but seemed to respond to "G," which was embroidered on his shirt –was climbing on chairs. At the moment, no one else seemed to be paying attention, so Brewer walked over.

"Be careful, don't fall from there," Brewer told him. "Do you want to go outside?"

Leewood – Brewer would later learn his name – stared back.

"Outside," he said. "Shoes."

Brewer found his shoes – a pair of black sneakers that looked brand-new – and put them on. Then she picked him up and carried him down a corridor and toward the front door.

As she walked, Brewer began to cry.

Outside, the sun was setting. Crickets were chirping.

Not too far away, a fountain gurgled.

"Do you want to get down and run?" she asked.

Leewood nodded, and she set him down.

"Do you hear those bugs?" she asked.

"Bugs," he said.

Brewer picked him up again and carried him to the fountain. He didn't want to get down, so she helped him reach a hand into the water.

Then they walked back inside.

Brewer had spent too long with the children already. "I rubbed the little baby on his belly," she said. "And I went back to work."

Chapter Ten
BIG BUDDIES

❀

Only three days after Hurricane Katrina struck the Gulf Coast, the Mall of Louisiana was open for business.

It was Thursday afternoon, and as tens of thousands of hurricane victims struggled to escape New Orleans, shoppers 80 miles to the west filed past Abercrombie & Fitch, Yankee Candle, and Victoria's Secret in Baton Rouge's biggest mall.

Lauren Billon, Jodi McKenzie and Derrick Robertson sat in the air-conditioned food court and shared an order of chicken fingers from Raising Cane's, a Louisiana fast-food chain famous for its special sauce.

The three had the day off because of Hurricane Katrina, and now they talked about finding a place to volunteer. Evacuees from New Orleans were pouring into the city, doubling the capital city's population in the space of a few days. Lauren, Jodi and Derrick – all in their 20s, all childless – suddenly had too much time on their hands.

Derrick's cell phone rang. It was Gaylynne Mack, their boss. Drop what you're doing, she said. There are 10 children stranded by the side of the road in New Orleans. Can you drive in and bring them back to Baton Rouge?

It's a dangerous job, she warned Derrick. "If you don't want to go, you don't have to," she said.

Derrick leapt up. "I'm gonna talk to y'all later," he said.

"Call us when you're close," Lauren and Jodi answered. "We'll make them dinner."

Maybe spaghetti, they thought.

Rescuing children from a hurricane-ravaged city certainly wasn't part of the usual Big Buddy job description.

Founded in 1979 by a Louisiana State University social-work teacher, Big Buddy started out as a mentoring program that matched adult volunteers with disadvantaged children. The non-profit group now serves 8,000 children in the Baton Rouge area. Although the mentoring program continues, Big Buddy workers and volunteers also tutor, supervise after-school activities, teach lessons in schools, and help fifth graders transition into middle school.

When Hurricane Katrina hit Louisiana, Big Buddy workers didn't immediately get involved. They weren't part of a formal emergency preparations plan, Mack said, but she and her employees quickly decided they wanted to help. On Thursday – the day the children were separated – Mack attended a meeting of the Baton Rouge United Way. The city's non-profit groups were trying to assess what could be done to help the thousands of New Orleans evacuees that were streaming into their city.

After the meeting, Melissa Flournoy, the head of the Louisiana Association of Non-Profits, approached Mack. Can we use your vans, she asked. We have a group of kids who are stranded in New Orleans. They need someone to pick them up.

Of course, Mack answered.

After hanging up with Mack, Derrick drove to the Big Buddy offices on Main Street in Baton Rouge, a 1960s-era office building that sits just a couple of blocks from Interstate 10. When he got there, his co-worker, Ursula Gold, was waiting for him in one of the program's vans.

With the images of looting and violence on the news, neither Derrick nor Ursula felt comfortable driving into New Orleans. But the image of 10 kids – 10 kids! – on the side of the interstate spurred them to action.

"In your mind you see this picture, like, 'Oh my God, what are those parents? Where are they?' You know, you're going crazy, like, 'Let's go!'" Derrick said.

Ursula, who is a mother of three, couldn't shake the image. "You couldn't imagine kids – *people*, period, on the side of the interstate – but *babies*, kids…."

Derrick navigated while Ursula drove. Not knowing what to expect made the drive doubly frightening. As the van rumbled over an elevated highway on the outskirts of New Orleans – Interstate 10 traverses swampy bayous and runs alongside Lake Pontchartrain before reaching the western suburb of Kenner – Ursula held her breath. She wondered if the hurricane might have ruptured the highway up ahead.

Every time they crested a hill, Ursula would say, "Ok, Derrick, where are we going?"

She also wondered where the hoards of evacuees were, not realizing she and Derrick were farther from New Orleans than she imagined. "I was just looking for all the people," she said.

Once the two reached the exit for the Louis Armstrong International Airport, they decided to check in to make sure that the rescuers were expecting them.

Ursula's cell phone had no signal, but Derrick managed to get through.

"We just sent to them to Baton Rouge in an ambulance," the voice on the other end of the line said.

"You sent them where?" Derrick asked in disbelief. Ursula turned the van around, and they drove back the way they had come.

Several phone calls later, Derrick and Ursula got their updated orders. Head to the Department of Health command center at Jimmy Swaggart Ministries, they were told. Pick up the kids and take them to the Louisiana State University field house, where workers had set up a special children-only shelter.

In Derrick and Ursula's worst-case imaginings, they somehow never pictured that their new charges would be toddlers and infants. Without specific information about the children's ages, they figured the kids were school-aged – a group that both were accustomed to working with at Big Buddy.

So they were stunned when they saw the children.

"They were seven of the most unimaginable ages," Derrick said.

Gabrielle – no one knew her name then – was asleep when they walked in, as was Dejahney, the girl everyone was calling Peanut. Zarione and Leewood raced around the room. De'Monté, having finished his broccoli, also couldn't sit still.

Derrick chased De'Monté around the room while Ursula set to work on the babies.

"We just started changing diapers and giving them bottles," she said. "Trying to quiet them."

Ursula's cell phone rang. It was Jodi. Are you close? she asked. When should we start dinner?

"We're changing diapers!" Ursula said. "These babies are on formula."

Jodi had been with Lauren at a Family Dollar, picking up supplies for the older kids that they had been planning for. Now they emptied their shopping cart and started throwing in diapers, blankets, bottles, underwear. "We were like, ok, change focus," Lauren said.

A spaghetti dinner was also out of the question, so they bought chicken fingers and other toddler-friendly food.

Some of the children had no shirts. Others had no shoes. The baby, however, had nearly everything he needed. "The baby's mom, she had all his stuff," Ursula said. "She had the baby's Pampers, she had little clothes, stuff like they were going for a little trip."

The only thing he was missing was formula.

The picture didn't make much sense. On the one hand, little Da'Roneal's bag had been carefully packed. The children were well behaved. One little boy – Leewood, whom everyone was calling G – was wearing new sneakers.

But what kind of parent would leave an infant on the side of the road? "I just thought, 'How dare these parents abandon their children?'" Derrick said.

Then he thought, "Are they dead?"

As Derrick and Ursula waited for Department of Health officials to release the children to their custody, Jodi and Lauren joined them. So did Ura, Ursula's sister.

Even though the children would get thorough medical exams when they arrived at the field house, no one wanted to take a chance on these kids. "They wouldn't let the kids go!" Ursula said.

Two hours later – by now, it was 9 or 10 p.m., well past the children's bedtime – an ambulance escorted the kids to the football locker room in LSU. Because the field house was being used as a shelter for the sick, the children had to be germ-free before they could enter.

Brent Broussard was waiting for them at the football locker room. Broussard, a 24-year-old salesman for a veterinarian supply company, had been helping out at the field house since the hurricane. As the doors to the ambulance opened, Brent saw Dejahney sitting on the ambulance driver's lap.

She stared back at him fearfully. Since being separated from Brian Sizemore, Dejahney had attached herself to a string of other people – mostly white men, for some reason – only to see them disappear.

Brent fit the profile. "I'll take her," he said.

"Be careful," someone warned. "She's going to hit you, and she spits."

As Brent took Dejahney into his arms, she flailed. "She hit me in the face about six times," he said.

They walked toward a ball field, away from the ambulance and the other children. He spoke softly. "I showed her the field and let her see the grass," he said. Soon, she stopped crying.

Once inside the locker room, the children went wild.

"Oh gosh!" Jodi said. "Those kids just took off."

Jodi and the others washed out the children's hair and scrubbed them as best they could under showers usually used by linebackers and tight ends.

With the exception of De'Monté.

"He didn't want to take a shower," Derrick said. Every time Derrick suggested it, in fact, De'Monté let out a high-pitched scream. By now, Ina Perkins, Big Buddy's office manager, had arrived to help. Together, Ina and Derrick tried to goad De'Monté into taking a bath.

"Yo, you gonna be cool if you take a bath," Derrick attempted.

"No," De'Monté answered.

Finally, Derrick grabbed a wet washcloth and wiped the boy down the best he could. He and the others dressed the children in LSU t-shirts and other clothes and took them to the field house.

The Carl Maddox Field House is a modern, two-story windowless building tucked between the Peter Maravich Assembly Center, the LSU tennis courts, and an outdoor track. In normal times, the field house is home to track meets and basketball games. Now, in the aftermath of Hurricane Katrina, it had been transformed into an infirmary for the sick and elderly. Cloth partitions divided the cavernous hall into sections – a triage area, a cafeteria, a dormitory. Outside, on the outdoor track, helicopters were landing every few minutes and unloading New Orleans' sickest evacuees. Workers admitted the most serious cases to the assembly center, which was being used as a temporary field hospital, while the stable patients were sent to convalesce in the field house.

In the days after the hurricane, elderly patients lay on cots, IVs in their arms, while the children of other patients played Chutes and Ladders or blocks with volunteers nearby. Some evacuees read the Bible on their cots. Others walked laps around the building's perimeter, or chatted with fellow patients on the bleachers.

On the field house's second floor, down a window-lined hallway overlooking the indoor track, the state's Department of Social Services had set up a children's shelter in what was normally the softball locker room.

To call the place a "locker room" doesn't really do it justice. "Clubhouse" might better describe the warren of rooms that was home to the softball team. In addition to lockers and showers, the amenities included a washer and dryer, as well as a kitchen sink, refrigerator and microwave. In one room, two leather couches flanked a big-screen TV. Action shots of the softball team and motivational posters – labeled "Challenge," "Vision" and "Dreams" – decorated the walls.

When the Big Buddy workers arrived late Thursday night with the children, the place had been transformed into a makeshift nursery. Mattresses and cribs filled the rooms, which were fully stocked with diapers and toys.

On the way up to the children's shelter, Derrick said goodbye to De'Monté.

"Okay," Derrick said. "Talk to you later." He was surprised to find himself fighting back tears.

"I'm never gonna leave you," De'Monté said.

Derrick looked at Ina, who was standing next to him. "Oh, Lord," he said.

"It was all over for Derrick, right there!" Ina recalled.

After Derrick left, the children played for a while, and Jodi took pictures of them with her camera phone. It was after midnight by the time the children finally went to sleep.

The rest of the Big Buddy workers parted ways. They'd already resolved to return first thing in the morning.

In the middle of the night, Derrick called Jodi.

"Can you e-mail me a picture of De'Monté?" he asked.

First thing Friday morning, the Big Buddy workers met at their office with Mack, the executive director. In addition to those who had cared for the children the day before, more workers had arrived. There was Kori Thomas, a mentor coordinator, and Terrell Thomas, who works in a program that helps fifth-graders transition into sixth grade. With thousands of evacuees continuing to pour in from New Orleans, Big Buddy's role was growing beyond the seven little children who were now sleeping in the LSU field house. Hundreds of kids were staying at the Baton Rouge River Center, a convention center that was being used as a makeshift shelter. Although those children were with their parents, they needed to be entertained.

Setting up activities for older children fit better within the traditional mission of Big Buddy. But those who had taken care of the stranded kids the night before didn't want to head to the River Center.

"We were trying to figure out how we were going to get to LSU!" Ursula said.

Finally, the director relented, and the Big Buddy workers headed to the field house. On the way there, they had loaded up on toys – balls, coloring books, board games.

Kori and some of the other newcomers got to work setting up a playroom in the outside hallway. Then the children woke up.

"It was like instant recognition," Jodi said.

It was 9 a.m. on Friday morning. It would be nearly midnight by the time the Big Buddy workers went home.

A pattern quickly developed. On Thursday evening, many of the children had bonded with one adult. Derrick, of course, had De'Monté. Ina gravitated toward Da'Roneal, with his saucer eyes. Jodi cared for Zarione, Lauren had Leewood, and Ura bonded with Ty're. That morning, Kori became close with Gabrielle.

"We kind of all had our own child," Jodi said.

Brent had returned that morning, too, to the relief of the others. Dejahney wasn't talking. When he arrived, he took her out to the track and got her to eat. "She wasn't eating with anyone else," Jodi said.

The workers quickly found that there were too many adults. "The kids were so bonded, like one to one, that it wasn't really like the kids were running around playing with multiple people," Kori said. "It was like one person was playing with them and when they were tired of playing, they wanted that one person to move to the next activity with them."

So Mack sent several of the newly arrived Big Buddy workers to the River Center and other areas of town.

Ursula and the others didn't budge. "We're fine here," she told Mack. "I'm not leaving."

Over the next few days, other children would arrive at the shelter. But there was something special about those seven.

"The other kids were older," Ursula said. "The other ones, they were happy to see us and they played, but you know they can eat on their own. They were independent… the babies, even though they had help, they didn't want the help from everybody else, they just wanted Big Buddy."

The Big Buddy workers were happy to oblige. "We were there when they woke up, we stayed with them the entire day and we put them to sleep," Jodi said. "And then we went home and the next day we did the same thing."

They sent others out to get lunch and bring it back to the shelter. Terrell drove to Old Navy and bought two outfits for each child.

The kids reveled in their fresh clothes. "They didn't want to take the stuff off," Ursula said.

Ura took out the braids in Ty're's hair and gave him new cornrows. "He had a new little attitude," Derrick said. "He ran around with his new little smile."

Derrick and the others were so consumed by the needs of the children, they nearly forgot about themselves. "We'd be like, oh my god, did we eat today?" Lauren recalled. "When did we get here?"

Many of the children began to see the workers as surrogate parents, a notion that both scared the adults and brought them closer to their charges. When the on-call night nurse made her final rounds, she relied on the Big Buddy workers to tell her where each child slept, or what they had eaten for the day.

On Saturday afternoon, Zarione developed a cough. Jodi called in a doctor and when he arrived, she woke Zarione from a nap. As she held her, the doctor asked, "How long have you been with her?" Jodi recalled.

"They became attached to you," Jodi said. "You knew what clothes were theirs, you knew what toys they liked to play with."

Some of the children began calling their female caretakers "Mama."

"And we'd be like, 'no, no!'" said Jodi. "We'd be like, 'no, I'm not mom!'"

When Leewood needed affection, he would walk up to Lauren and say, "Hold me, Mama," Lauren recalled. "It would break your heart."

In moments like this, the Big Buddy workers wondered what had happened to their parents. What would make a mother give up her children?

Through De'Monté, they were starting to get a better picture.

By Friday, Derrick and De'Monté had developed a playful bond. Derrick broached the subject gently.

"Wow, you were on the side of the street?" he asked the boy.

"Yep," De'Monté answered.

"Well, where was your mama?" Derrick asked. "Your mama just left you?"

"No," De'Monté said.

"Well, what happened?"

"We were on the roof," De'Monté said.

Derrick pulled the story out in one- and two-word answers. De'Monté and the children took a helicopter. It was scary. His mama didn't come with them. She cried.

"When you got to the side of the street, what happened?" Derrick asked.

Just then, De'Monté found a toy to play with. The interview was over.

Over the next day, De'Monté would occasionally talk about his parents, or his house, or his school. Once, the boy looked at Derrick and said, "Darryl?"

"What?" Derrick asked.

"Darryl? Darryl Williams?"

"I'm not Darryl Williams," Derrick said.

"I know," De'Monté said. "That's my daddy's name."

Another time, De'Monté recited his phone number. Derrick decided it couldn't hurt to try. When he dialed the number, of course, the call didn't go through.

Some of the little ones also divulged hints about their pasts.

Zarione knew her name. She could tell the workers she was from New Orleans.

At first, they didn't know that she and Ty're were sister and brother. From De'Monté, they knew the children were his cousins, but nothing more.

Then they noticed that when Zarione and Ty're went to sleep, they insisted on sleeping next to each other. "When they would get up in the morning, they would look for each other," Jodi said.

Once, Zarione told Jodi that she wanted to see her brother.

"Who's your brother?" Jodi asked.

"Ty're," she answered.

Although the children played and slept and cuddled with their caregivers, there was no substitute for their real parents.

Each night, Leewood cried himself to sleep. "I want my Mama," he would blubber, over and over.

Lauren, lying next to him on the floor, cried along with him.

"All of them would be fine until – like any kids – it came close to the time to go home," Ursula said. "At some time in the day, they were like, 'ok, it's time to go home.'"

Zarione, normally a happy child, would abruptly switch moods.

"She would just stop and she would just stare," Jodi recalled.

"Zaria?" Jodi would ask. "Zaria, are you okay?"

"NO!" she'd scream, and take off running. Then, just like that, she'd snap out of it.

No one was sure how much time would pass before the parents showed up. On Friday, Lauren called an elementary school she works with at Big Buddy and asked if they would let De'Monté attend.

If Monday came and the children still hadn't been reunited with their parents, the system would have to change. Big Buddy, which had closed its doors since the hurricane's arrival, would begin offering its regular programs again, and everyone would have to go back to work.

At one point, they wondered if they could set up the nursery at the Big Buddy office. "We were trying to figure out how these kids, how we were still going to be involved in their lives, after we had to go back to work," Jodi said.

The Big Buddy workers knew the real solution was to find the children's parents. But in a sea of evacuees – a historic movement of people, who were now scattered to nearly every state in the nation – how would they ever succeed?

Chapter Eleven
SAFETY, BUT NOT SOLACE

As the airplane descended toward San Antonio, Catrina Williams daydreamed of a hot shower, good food and a bed.

It was late morning on Friday, September 2, four days since Hurricane Katrina. Even before they left the apartment, sleep had been hard to come by because of the heat. "We were just exhausted," she said.

Twenty-four hours had passed since Catrina had put her children on a helicopter. Now, she wondered if they might be waiting for her in San Antonio.

The scene at Kelly Air Field, the former Air Force base where the plane landed a few minutes later, looked more like a bus depot than an airport. Dozens of buses lined up on the tarmac, and Catrina, Felecia and the rest of the crew boarded one of them. A short ride later, it stopped in front of Building 171, an empty office building that the city had converted into a shelter. It was an unromantic name for the place they were to call home for the next several weeks.

When the mothers arrived that Friday, the enormity of the evacuation was just beginning to dawn on the people of San Antonio.

Only the night before, the Houston Astrodome had closed its doors to new evacuees after accepting up to 15,000 people. That day, Keith Berger, the Red Cross' shelter operations manager for San Antonio, got a phone call. Get ready for up to 25,000 evacuees, he was told. San Antonio just got named one of the storm's major evacuation hubs.

"They were looking at going big," Berger said. Before then, the Red Cross had been operating two small shelters – one in a high school and one in a middle school – for the few hurricane evacuees who had trickled into San Antonio on their own. Now, Berger and his colleagues were considering bigger locations, such as the Freeman Coliseum, a concert and events venue, and an empty Montgomery Ward store in the Windsor Park Mall. City officials offered several empty buildings at KellyUSA, the former airfield that the city was now promoting as a business and industrial park.

By Friday morning, Berger and his colleagues had designated Building 171, a mammoth one-story office building that stretched the length of an entire city block at KellyUSA, as San Antonio's primary shelter. The building wasn't ideal. It had no public address system, no showers, and the interior consisted of a maze of low, gray hallways that led to windowless offices.

The Red Cross got to work clearing the building of its contents, then transforming it into a miniature city. Workers built showers outside, while others set up cots and installed desks, phone lines and computers. In the beginning, Red Cross workers divided the building into a giant intake area, a feeding area, and three sleeping areas.

When the first droves of evacuees arrived at around 11 a.m. Friday, "it took us off guard a little bit," Berger said. Not only were they getting planeloads of people such as Catrina and Felecia, but buses that had been turned away from the Houston Astrodome also pulled up to Building 171. Berger had trained for massive shelters because San Antonio is designated as an evacuation point for hurricanes that hit Corpus Christi, which is 150 miles southeast of the city. But he was still overwhelmed.

"They were starving, they wanted to eat," he said. "Then they came back and wanted showers."

Catrina, Felecia and the other mothers were no different, but first they wanted their children. "We lost our kids," they told officials as they waited in line, hoping that they would be moved to the front. No luck.

After an hours-long wait, Catrina and her father, Adrian, checked in at the medical center to see if they could get new prescriptions for their diabetes medication.

The nurse asked a couple of questions, and took Catrina's temperature. She took her blood pressure.

"Stand up," the nurse said. She took Catrina's blood pressure standing up.

"Now sit down again," she said. Again, she took her blood pressure.

The next thing she knew, Catrina was speeding through San Antonio in the back of an ambulance, bound for Methodist Hospital. Her blood pressure was dangerously high, the medical workers had told her as they lowered her onto a stretcher.

The news puzzled Catrina. "I don't suffer from high blood pressure," she protested. Ever since the hurricane began, she had been battling a terrible headache. But she had written it off as related to the stress.

Now, as the ambulance raced through an unfamiliar city, she worried about Darryl. While waiting for the nurse to see her, Darryl had left to get her some dinner. Now, he had no idea where she was. In fact, no one did.

Back at Building 171, the others tried to get their bearings. There was a line for everything, it seemed – a shower, a meal, even a bed. And everywhere, people wandered aimlessly, unsure of where they were supposed to be.

Adding to the confusion was the fact that many volunteers and government workers arrived at the same time as the evacuees. "It was chaotic," said Melissa Tijerina, a program director for the Texas Child Protective Services agency. "There were just people everywhere."

Somewhere inside Building 171, Sherri Montez moved through the crowd.

She didn't work for any agency. She wasn't affiliated with either the Red Cross or the Salvation Army.

She was a rogue volunteer.

Earlier that day, Montez had been sitting in a Costco store, filling out a job application. She was a single mother of two teenagers, and unemployed. She had once made a living as a film production coordinator, but had been jobless ever since San Antonio's film industry bottomed out.

The television in Costco's employee area was on, and Montez watched it out of the corner of her eye. As images of New Orleans flashed across the screen, Montez thought to herself, "What am I doing here?" She needed the money, but "whatever my problems were, they were nothing compared to what these people were going through."

Before she knew it, Montez was driving her Mazda 3 toward KellyUSA, unsure of what she would do when she got there. When she had called the Red Cross, the person who answered the phone said they didn't need any more volunteers. Leave us your number, and the volunteer coordinator will get back to you, Montez was told. The story was the same when she had called the Salvation Army. Don't come, they told her. You'll be wasting your time.

"They're crazy," Montez said to herself. "I know better than that."

As she walked toward the front doors of Building 171, Montez reminded herself of one of her mother's favorite lessons. "No matter where you're going, act like you're supposed to be there."

Montez walked confidently through the doors. No one stopped her.

She started by walking up to evacuees. She went first to the ones who were crying.

"How can I help you?" she'd ask. "What are you trying to find?"

Some people asked her for a ride to the airport. Others needed a bus ticket to another city. "I thought, well, they need that," Montez said. "They have food, they have shelter, they have basic needs, but a lot of them want to be with their families."

Montez wandered some more, exploring. She walked down the hallways, opening doors. Eventually, she found an empty office. She borrowed a piece of paper and a pen from someone.

"Transportation Office," she wrote, and hung the sign on the door. She had no fax, no computer, not even a landline. Just an outdated Nokia cell phone and a sense of purpose. Sherri Montez had just appointed herself the transportation coordinator for KellyUSA.

While the Red Cross and FEMA were handling the major movements of people, Berger – the Red Cross shelter coordinator – acknowledged that they did not arrange for smaller travel needs. Because of the potential danger of driving strangers in people's own cars, Berger said Red Cross volunteers were discouraged from doing the work themselves. "We were being very careful not to condone that because of the safety aspect," Berger said.

Montez disregarded the warnings. On one of the trips, she managed to fit six people in her Mazda. But every time she returned to her new office, there was a crowd of people waiting for her. I need help, she thought. So she wandered over to the Red Cross volunteer station.

Like Montez, others had disregarded the advice of the Red Cross and simply shown up at Building 171, ready to help. Berger, the shelter coordinator, said the Red Cross simply couldn't keep up with the number of people willing to help. Because of the long Labor Day weekend, everyone had time off. "I had groups of 500 people showing up at the shelter wanting to volunteer," Berger said. "We had so many volunteers, we just couldn't find jobs for them to do. They were becoming a problem, just trying to keep up with the volunteers."

Now, some of those volunteers milled about the Red Cross station, waiting for an assignment. Montez sized up her unwitting job candidates. She didn't need a follower. "I needed people that no matter what it was, if we needed to get it done, we're gonna get it done."

Then she spotted Shannon Cantrell. Like Montez, Cantrell had ignored the advice of Red Cross workers and shown up anyway at KellyUSA. With a long weekend off from her job in economic development for Texas Governor Rick Perry, Cantrell and her husband, a nurse, decided to see if they could help out. "We thought, 'we know they're going to need people," Cantrell said. Sure enough, as soon as they arrived, the Red Cross gave them a five-minute training briefing and set them to work.

Montez met Cantrell when she was waiting for an assignment.

"She looks like a go-getter," Montez said to herself. Cantrell had something about her that Montez liked. "You could see it in her eyes. She had the drive and the heart," Sherri said.

Cantrell, too, saw something in Montez. "She was such a dynamo," she said. With Cantrell's background in politics and Montez' experience in film production, the two were used to making things happen. "It was a natural fit," Cantrell said.

As Montez and Cantrell set to work, Catrina lay in a hospital bed 10 miles away.

Someone had given her a t-shirt and a pair of scrubs to change into, and some fuzzy slippers to cover her feet. Catrina threw out the clothes she was wearing; she had become so detested with them that she can no longer describe what they looked like.

After she had arrived, a nurse had taken her blood pressure and a doctor ordered more tests. She ate a sandwich – "I don't know what kind it was, but I know it was good because I ate it all," she said – and had something to drink. There were cookies, too, and Jell-O. "It was pretty decent," she said.

For the first time in nearly a week, Catrina lay in an air-conditioned room.

When the tears started, she couldn't stop them.

"I want my kids," she said, over and over.

"I felt so empty," Catrina said. "I felt like, you know what? Why am I going through this? Why are we going through this second tragedy?"

She prayed to God. "Please, let my kids be all right."

As she cried, she began to doubt her decision to push her kids on the helicopter. At the same time, she didn't know what other choice she could have made. "Where we was at, what could we give them? Nothing but more heartache and pain. There was nothing to offer them."

Catrina spilled her pain to the doctor. "All we want is our kids," she said.

In addition to a prescription for her diabetes and blood pressure, the doctor wrote her one for anxiety.

As Catrina showered later, she overheard the doctor as he passed by her room. "We need to get Miss Williams her kids back," the doctor told his companion. "Do whatever you can. This lady needs her kids."

Chapter Twelve
ADAM'S TEAM

From his living room in Terre Haute, Indiana, Joe Newport cycled through the news channels like everybody else. CNN. Fox. MSNBC.

It was Thursday, Sept. 1, and the full scale of the devastation in New Orleans was beginning to dawn on newscasters and the American public alike. There were plenty of people to worry about – the sick who were stranded in hospitals, the elderly who were trapped at the Superdome, and the thousands of others who were still stuck on rooftops, waiting for helicopters.

Joe Newport worried about the children.

He picked up the phone and dialed the Alexandria, Virginia headquarters of the National Center for Missing and Exploited Children.

Brenda Galarza, his boss, answered her line.

What can I do? Newport asked. He knew that the center had already activated its Project Alert, a volunteer program that calls on retired law enforcement officials to assist in abducted children cases. Now, at the request of the Department of Justice, the center was in the midst of setting up a special hotline and getting ready to serve as the main clearinghouse for children and adults lost in Hurricane Katrina. Newport volunteered to answer hotline calls.

But Galarza had other plans for him. We're deploying Team Adam, she said. How soon can you get to Baton Rouge?

Around the same time, nearly 1,000 miles southwest of Terre Haute, Michael Keller's phone rang in his home in Aransas Pass, Texas.

Team Adam has been activated, said Larry Upchurch, the unit's director and Galarza's boss. You're going to Baton Rouge.

Since Monday, Keller had been asking for just that. As a retired police chief, he couldn't bear to see fellow officers struggling in what everyone now realized was one of the biggest natural disasters in the nation's history. "There's got to be something we can do," he told his bosses at the center.

Now, he had his wish.

Team Adam is an elite corps of retired law enforcement officials – cops, detectives, search-and-rescue experts, police chiefs – who are trained to swoop into town whenever local police need help with a missing-kid case.

The team's creation in 2003 fulfilled a longtime goal of the National Center for Missing and Exploited Children. The center's mission – to prevent child abduction and sexual exploitation, to help find missing children, and to assist victims – was inspired by the death of Adam Walsh, the 6-year-old boy who was kidnapped from a shopping mall in 1981 and later murdered. The case won national attention and his parents – Revé and John Walsh, the host of the "America's Most Wanted" television show – helped found the National Center in 1984.

Some of the center's best-known initiatives are its national missing-children hotline and its advocacy for the Amber Alert system, a nationwide emergency alert system that goes into effect in high-risk child kidnapping cases.

For two decades, the center had been providing valuable data to local police departments in missing-children cases. Using donated databases of public records, experts at the National Center could quickly profile possible suspects, inundating departments with a list of their present and past addresses, possible relatives, other aliases and motor-vehicle registration records.

Technicians at the National Center had also become proficient at a technology known as "age progression" – the computerized alteration of missing-kids photographs when cases have gone unsolved for years. Through collaboration with the U.S. Secret Service, the center also had access to handwriting analysis, lie detectors, fingerprint searches, and other forensic tools.

But for years, officials at the National Center wanted to do more. They were particularly concerned about what they call "stereotypical kidnapping" cases. While the Department of Justice reports that non-family members abduct about 58,200 children each year, only in about 115 cases is a child taken more than 50 miles from home, held overnight, held for ransom, or killed.

In those cases, time is of the essence. One study cited by the National Center shows that in 74 percent of child abduction cases, the victim is murdered within three hours of being kidnapped. Many times, the Center says, kidnappers who sexually assault or murder children are repeat offenders. What's more, departments can be overwhelmed when the cases become media events, their every move scrutinized by reporters around the country.

But because such scenarios occur relatively infrequently, most police departments will encounter one only once in a generation. As a police officer or detective in a small department, said Galarza, Team Adam's assistant project manager, "You'll never actually work a true non-family abduction case. To us, handling these cases all around the United States, we knew we had some investigative experience."

So with a $3 million grant from the Michael and Susan Dell Foundation – the charitable foundation of the computer executive – the National Center launched Team Adam, named for Adam Walsh. "We tried to come up with a name that meant something to this organization and also to the United States," Galarza said.

The plan was simple. Much like the National Transportation and Safety Board deploys a team of experts to the scene just hours after a plane crash or other major accident, Team Adam would send missing-kids specialists to the site of serious abduction cases. Once there, the team members – usually a pair – would help local law enforcement and serve as a liaison to family members.

The National Center set a high bar for its Team Adam consultants. Candidates had to be retired from a law enforcement agency, and they had to have experience investigating child-abduction cases. Other requirements included running a command post in a major incident, working with other jurisdictions, and experience interviewing witnesses, Galarza said.

Joe Newport, then, was an ideal candidate. He had retired in 1999 from the Terre Haute police department after 23 years on the force. His career had included six years as the department's chief of detectives, and four as chief of police. Because of the department's small size – about 140 officers – investigators worked all kinds of cases. "It was general assignment," Newport said. "From thefts to homicides and everything in between."

In a city of 70,000, Newport relished being a small-town police officer. "I think you really become a cop to help people at all levels," he said. "Not just in terrible murder cases but also if you meet somebody that needs directions in the city, you take the time and you be kind."

Then, in 1986, Newport got a big-city case. That October, the family of 17-year-old Alicia Elmore reported that their daughter had disappeared after going to the store to buy some soda. The following February, she was discovered alive, stuffed into a ceiling crawl space in the home of Bill Benefiel, Jr. For four months, Alicia had been chained naked to a bed and raped dozens of times. Benefiel had glued her eyes shut, shoved toilet paper into her mouth and cut her with a knife.

Two weeks before she was discovered, Benefiel brought home a second girl – 18-year-old Dolores Wells. He chained her to a bed, too, then superglued her nostrils shut and shoved toilet paper down her throat. Benefiel left the home for a few hours and when he returned home, told Alicia he had killed Delores. When police later knocked on his door, he stuffed Alicia into the crawl space.

"It almost sounds like one of those detective magazine stories, but it really was that terrible," Newport said.

Newport's detective work helped police arrest Benefiel days later. With the help of Alicia's testimony, Benefiel was sentenced to death in 1988. He was finally executed in April of 2005.

After the Benefiel case, Newport traveled to National Center headquarters to take a course for investigators in missing-children cases. The center's resources and goals blew him away. "It was remarkable," he said. "And I really bought into the program."

Too often, Newport said, detectives complete a case and move on to the next without looking back. "But the National Center's focus is all about the kids," Newport said. As he sat in the class, he listened to the instructors talk about counseling and finding ways to make the children as whole as possible after such traumatic events. "It was from their heart and from their soul," he said. "They really believe in that. So gosh, who can deny that?"

When Newport became chief of the Terre Haute police department, he took a course for executives. Then, after retiring, he volunteered for the Project Alert program. But while he was in training, he learned about the center's new Team Adam.

Newport's wife had recently died of breast cancer. "I had more time than I cared to have," he said. His four children were in their early 20s and nearly grown. Even though Newport had a job, as the associate director of public safety at Indiana State University, he had flexibility.

"I can pick up and go," he said.

Like Newport, Keller is a retired police chief. He served for 32 years on the force of Webster, a Houston suburb. For the last five years of his career, he was its police chief. Like Newport, Keller first became interested in the National Center after his department worked the case of a missing child: Amber Griffin, a 9-year-old girl who was kidnapped allegedly by a family friend in 1998 and later found alive.

While attending a class for police chiefs, Keller learned about Project Alert, and how participants do community outreach, work cold cases, and answer hotline calls when a child goes missing. "I was very interested in it, but you had to be retired," he said.

So when Keller retired in 2001, he got back in touch with the National Center.

"I am 100 percent cop," Keller said. "I was having some difficulty dealing with retirement. This was an opportunity to stay in policing without being a police chief."

After serving on Project Alert for a few years, Keller applied to Team Adam. He joined their ranks in 2004.

In its first two years of operation, Team Adam kept busy. By October of 2005, the National Center had activated the team members a total of 203 times, sending its members to 41 states. Because some of the cases involved multiple children, the deployments involved 230 children, 212 of whom were found, Galarza said. All but 42 of those children were found alive.

Team Adam members rushed to the scene in the case of Lindsey Ryan, a 14-year-old girl from Jones, Michigan who was kidnapped in March 2003 by a convicted murderer. She was later recovered. They also helped on the case of 11-year-old Shakira Johnson, a Cleveland girl who was kidnapped near her house in 2003. She was later found raped and murdered.

Newport, Keller and other Team Adam members take their lead from the local police department. "We make great pains to not take over the investigation. That's not our purpose," Newport said. Often, he said, he serves as an advisor and a liaison between the department and the family. "The victim's family, they want a benevolent side of the police that maybe is not so evident sometimes…And their feelings get hurt."

A missing-kid case quickly overwhelms even a medium-size police department, said Keller. Often, the kidnappings become a media event. "These kids can make or break their careers," Keller said. In addition, a department can bust its budget in the search. With all these issues playing out behind the scenes, Keller said, it's nice to have the advice of experts who have been through it before.

In addition to public-information databases the National Center provides, they can also offer other resources. In one recent case, Keller was sent to Nacogdoches, Texas to help find a 22-month-old boy who had been missing for three weeks. Knowing that most young children are found close to home, Keller and the other Team Adam members recommended searching some woods near the boy's house.

They called the National Center and had them send a pair of specially trained cadaver dogs to aid in the search. His body turned up within 24 hours. "We have a wealth of resources and expertise that's unparalleled," Keller said.

When Hurricane Katrina hit, it was just those resources that the Department of Justice hoped to tap. The National Center has a relationship with the justice department that dates to its inception, when the organization was founded as part of the 1984 Missing Children's Assistance Act. In 2004, the justice department provided $30 million in funding, in addition to the $16 million the non-profit takes in from private contributions.

Although there were no reports of abducted children, National Center officials quickly decided to deploy Team Adam to the hurricane's hotspots. By Friday, September 2, Galarza and Upchurch had dispatched more than a dozen Team Adam members to five locations – Gulfport, Mississippi, Montgomery, Alabama, Houston, Baton Rouge, and San Antonio.

Michael Keller was the first to arrive in Baton Rouge, having driven the eight hours from his Texas home in a rental car. Keller didn't expected to find many missing children. Instead, he was hoping to help the hundreds of New Orleans police officers who had been working around the clock, despite the fact that most had lost their own homes in the floods.

"No one anticipated the extent of what was going on," Keller said.

Keller's instructions were to head to Baton Rouge, and check in at the Department of Social Services' emergency operations center.

When he arrived on Thursday afternoon, the scene was chaotic. "This was an event that was overwhelming to all state agencies," he said. "They were struggling."

The hurricane's aftermath had upended all of the social service agency's normal routines, said Rhenda Hodnett, assistant director of program development for the state DSS.

In normal times, the agency can't just take custody of a child – an investigation is needed to determine if a child is abused or neglected. Confidentiality is paramount. But in post-Katrina Louisiana, none of that applied. Few of the cases they were confronting involved abuse or neglect, and no judges were available to decide cases, anyway. Rather than keeping the details of cases secret, Hodnett and her colleagues now found themselves approaching the media for help in finding the parents.

To an agency accustomed to adhering to practices and procedures, the change was disorienting. "Just everything we normally do, all the confidentiality issues, all of that, really had to be thought through quite differently," she said.

Keller, a cop's cop, had little patience for the officials' bureaucratic debates. "They needed somebody to come in and take charge," he said. "I have no problem doing that."

The retired police chief quickly went into "incident management" mode, trying to determine what the highest priority issues were, and then finding a way to solve them.

By the next morning, Newport had joined him, arriving on a plane from Indianapolis. Like Keller, he was surprised at the disarray that greeted him. "I think somebody said, 'Glad you're here, don't know what to tell you what to do, but get busy,'" Newport said.

Keller and Newport learned that several young children had been brought to the agency's children-only shelter at the LSU field house overnight. "We decided we'd set up shop over there," Keller said. "We'd make sure the kids were okay, and then set up a process by which we can get them reunited with their parents."

Despite the chaos of the hurricane, Newport and Keller had a surprising number of resources already available to them. Keller had a digital camera, and both men had Dell laptops and cell phones provided by the National Center. And because the LSU campus is outfitted with wireless Internet access, they could also go online.

The men commandeered a couple of tables and set up them up in the hallway outside the children's shelter. One of them fashioned a sign out of a piece of paper. The Baton Rouge office of the National Center for Missing and Exploited Children was open for business.

By Friday, a few more children had trickled into the shelter, but most were older children – 9- and 10-year-olds and even a few teenagers. What caught Newport's eye was the group of seven children. The children were so young – a baby, five toddlers, and a six-year-old boy. Keller, who was acting as the scene commander, assigned Newport the case.

With the exception of De'Monté, none of the other children could say their names.

"A lot of these kids, of course, they're pretty upset and they're screaming their little heads off," Newport said. "It's hard to get any kind of semblance of order."

Keller understood why the children couldn't say their names, but it didn't make it any less frustrating. "They're separated from their parents, they've gone through this hurricane, now they're with a bunch of strangers," he said. "They were shy and withdrawn. These are things you would expect out of these children."

Because the Big Buddy workers had developed such a close rapport with the kids, Newport relied on them to do most of the interviewing. With Derrick's help, Newport learned many of the details De'Monté had provided, but he wasn't sure whether to trust the information.

"No one really knew if he understood all the questions," Newport said. Complicating matters was the name De'Monté kept giving for his mother. It just happened to match the name of the hurricane he had just survived.

"He'd say 'Catrina' and we thought. 'Well, hell, is all the things he's been telling us bullshit, or what? Is he confused?'" Newport said.

Newport and Keller decided their best shot was to get the children photographed and posted on the National Center's website.

One by one, the Big Buddy workers lined up with their children. As Keller took each photograph, Newport copied what little information they had on the child onto a makeshift form, which he planned to fax to the National Center.

Lauren settled one of the two-year-olds on her lap as Keller got ready to snap her picture. She wasn't one of De'Monté's cousins, and no one was sure of her name. The girl had seven braids in her hair and had arrived in a flowered t-shirt and a pair of blue shorts. The Big Buddy workers had taken to calling her Tiger.

Keller snapped the photo. Then he got an idea, and flipped the electronic screen around. "Who's that?" he asked the girl.

Tiger snatched the camera from his hand and cackled. "That's Gabby!" she said.

Lauren and Kori exchanged looks. "Oh my God," Lauren said.

Newport made a note on his information sheet. "Possibly named Gabby," he wrote.

Chapter Thirteen
THE SEARCH BEGINS

While Catrina lay in a hospital bed across town, the rest of the mothers began the search – again – for their children.

After what seemed like an hours-long wait to be processed at the San Antonio shelter, volunteers copied down their names, social security numbers, and home addresses. Then they passed out pink wristbands and assigned them a cot. At each step of the way, the mothers made their plea: Help us find our children.

Finally, after threading their way through a labyrinth of cubicles, the women arrived at "Missing Persons," which was being run by Texas Child Protective Services.

The state employees were still setting up when the women arrived. For a reason no one could explain, the Red Cross had assigned the agency a cubicle inside the shelter's mental health unit. The spot was so hard to get to that instead of giving directions by cell phone to newly arriving colleagues, CPS program director Melissa Tijerina walked to the front entrance and guided them back herself.

"It was crazy," Tijerina said. "These were the first people being processed in here, so no one was familiar with where everything was going to be."

Tijerina's colleague, Ben Hernandez, took down the mothers' information.

What are their names? What do they look like? Do they have any unusual physical attributes, like a scar, a missing tooth? When was the last time you saw them? What happened?

Most of the women seemed in a daze, Hernandez said. "They weren't really very emotional," he said. "They were just physically and emotionally exhausted."

Tijerina, however, remembers that one of the women could barely speak. The woman was likely Yowanda, because Tijerina remembers that she called her son Dooda, a nickname for Leewood.

"One of our first questions was what do your kids look like, and she could barely even talk about it," Tijerina said.

By that time, Yowanda and Marcie were crying nearly all the time. "I wondered where my baby was at," Yowanda said. "Is he warm? Is he safe? Is he eating?"

Also listening in was Paul Burke, a Team Adam consultant who had arrived just hours earlier from his home in Carson City, Nevada.

As a former search-and-rescue specialist for the Alaska State Police, an office building in sweltering San Antonio was an unlikely spot for Burke to be plying his trade.

In his 20 years as a state trooper, Burke ran an eight-member team that conducted more than 500 searches a year – ranging from stranded hikers, hunters and snowmobile riders to kidnapped children. Because of the state's unforgiving climate, "you have to work quickly and have good resources," Burke said. "I don't want to sound like you have to be smarter, but you have to do things that count."

In 2001, Burke retired from the force and moved to the arid climes of Nevada. He joined Team Adam in February of 2005, after a friend suggested he apply. By the time he arrived in San Antonio that Friday, September 2, Burke had already worked about a dozen cases for the National Center, including some that became national stories.

Just weeks after joining Team Adam, for example, Burke traveled to Homosassa, Florida to help investigators search for Jessica Lunsford, the 9-year-old girl who was abducted from her bed and later killed, allegedly by a sex offender who lived on her street.

Burke had been in Alaska, teaching a search-and-rescue class, when the National Center asked him to help with the Hurricane Katrina aftermath. "I came home, packed my bag, and went down to San Antonio," he said.

Burke is used to scaling mountains and searching the tundra for his victims, but the scene he encountered at KellyUSA was challenging in a different way.

"The place was just a madhouse," Burke said. When he got to the missing persons cubicle, there were no power outlets, no computers, no phone lines, no lights, and no chairs.

Evacuees quickly encircled anyone with an official look about them. "You were inundated," he said. Everyone had someone who was missing.

"I can't work here," Burke told the Red Cross organizers.

Finally, the Red Cross moved CPS and Burke to their own office later that night – Room 311, a windowless room not far from the shelter's three sleeping areas.

Early Saturday morning, Burke interviewed the women again. By this time, Catrina had joined the group.

Hospital workers had returned her to KellyUSA hours earlier, when she had run into Darryl in the hallway.

He was pacing back and forth, and smoking "like a choo-choo train," Catrina remembers.

"Where you at?" Darryl asked her. As she clutched her bag of newly prescribed drugs for high blood pressure and anxiety, Catrina recounted the story.

A night's sleep and some hot food had improved everyone's mood.

"While they weren't completely calm," Burke said, "they had a fair amount of control." Maybe it was because for the first time in two days, someone was looking for the kids in earnest. "They knew people were working on this."

The fact that the women stuck together also must have helped, he said. "I saw on occasion, when one would get upset, the other would console her," he said. Other parents were left to face their fear alone, in a sea of strangers. "This family was able to support one another, and I thought that worked out really well for them."

As Burke interviewed the mothers, Sherri Montez and her newly recruited assistant, Shannon Cantrell, struggled to keep up with demand.

Not even 24 hours had passed since Montez and Cantrell had hung a sign outside a vacant room and set up KellyUSA's transportation office.

Without official sponsorship by the Red Cross or FEMA, the two had to get creative about finding funds. They e-mailed friends and convinced them to donate frequent flier miles. Someone walked into the office with 400 dollars in cash he had collected at work. A rancher wandered by and donated $5,000.

Because she couldn't buy bus tickets over the phone, Montez spent much of her time Friday driving back and forth to the station, where she would stand in long lines for tickets. By Saturday morning, Montez had convinced a local church to donate its van and bus, along with two drivers. The men set to work ferrying evacuees to and from the hospital, bus station and airport.

In order to avoid problems with security guards, who were restricting access to authorized volunteers only, Montez walked over to the Red Cross station and grabbed a sticker that said "Volunteer." She slapped it on her shirt.

Word spread quickly about Montez and her transportation office. One morning – Montez is not sure when, since many of the days blended together inside the windowless offices – she showed up to find a crowd of 300.

As she and Cantrell struggled to find out what each person needed, those waiting in line began to complain. What's the holdup? They asked. Some even started shouting. Wiping away tears, Montez stood on a chair and addressed the crowd.

"I'm trying to do all I can," she said. "I'm just a single mom. I'm not *with* anybody."

When she stopped talking, "everybody just got real quiet," she said.

The rogue volunteer was gaining a reputation as a go-to woman.

"The people knew that if they came to our office, if they needed to find out something, we would help them find out whatever it was they needed to know," Montez said.

The idea amused her. "Here's a single mom, unemployed, and they're coming to her?" she said, laughing. "And then when FEMA started sending people and the Red Cross, I was like, 'Oh my God, I can't believe it.'"

One of those who sought Montez's help was Paul Burke.

By Saturday, Burke and the CPS workers could barely keep up with recording new cases, let alone get started on reuniting families.

"The sheer magnitude – the numbers – it was very overwhelming," Burke said. "You take one case, you start to work it, and you get three."

Once offered a sympathetic ear, many of the evacuees wouldn't stop talking. "They wanted to tell you their life story," he said. With some regret, Burke was forced to cut them off, and instead just take down names and the basic details of their case. Without working computers, Burke and the others recorded the information on makeshift forms and stuffed them in a big three-ring notebook, alphabetized by the parents' last names. By Saturday, the binder was bulging at its seams.

"It was very much a triage situation," he said.

Burke called Montez his "silent soldier."

On Saturday morning, Burke had very little resources at his disposal. Unlike his counterparts in Baton Rouge, who had wireless

Internet access and fax machines, Burke had no phone lines, no Internet access. Montez saw to everything. At one point – when there was a problem with Burke's business credit card – she even convinced a friend to buy him a photocopier.

"If you tell her 'I need six green chairs,' she'd find six green chairs," Burke said. "For her to eliminate some of those stresses for us, that allowed us to do our work in getting this match made."

As Burke copied down the mothers' information, he decided to make the case of the seven children one of his priorities. Some of the situations were virtually unsolvable, at least for the moment. If a parent was separated from a single child, Burke had little to offer. "When they land somewhere," he told them, "and they get on a register, we'll search the registers daily."

But these children and these mothers were different. Because the children had been taken in a single helicopter, "we got the feeling they were going to be all together, and probably wouldn't have been split up," he said. "We were hoping and praying that nobody separated the children any further."

Only a day earlier, a mental health counselor had told Marcie that her children were safe in Baton Rouge. But by Saturday, that important clue had gotten lost in the jumble of broken promises and debunked rumors. If Marcie told anyone in San Antonio that the children were in Baton Rouge, no one remembers.

Instead, workers copied her information onto an intake form.

"Mother: Marceline Alexander," the form read.

"Child: Gabrielle."

Chapter Fourteen
"WE HAVE A MATCH"

The world headquarters of the National Center for Missing and Exploited Children sits on the corner of Prince and Washington streets in Alexandria, in a neighborhood clogged with other non-profits looking to bend the ear of policymakers in nearby Washington, D.C.

From the outside, the onetime hotel maintains the stately elegance of the 1920s, when it was built. But inside, 21st century technology fills the five-story building, which became the National Center's headquarters in 1999 thanks to a $5 million donation by Computer Associates executive Charles B. Wang.

Three hundred employees sit at state-of-the-art computers that are hooked into an international network run on a powerful Sun Microsystems server.

Hotline workers answer phones 24 hours a day and have access to translators in 140 languages. Each call is analyzed and prioritized, then sent to a team of National Center case managers, as well as to state missing-children clearinghouses around the country.

With just a handful of keystrokes, National Center investigators can search a database of more than 2,200 children. In minutes, workers can send photographs of a missing child to hundreds of locations nationwide. During Amber Alerts, the National Center zaps descriptions of the child to thousands of cell phones and e-mail inboxes in targeted geographic areas.

On an average day, workers at the National Center for Missing and Exploited Children keep busy. Last year, the group handled 81,787 missing-child cases. Investigators in the center's Internet crime section receive 300 reports a day of crimes against children.

On Friday, September 2, the center was busier than ever.

While Team Adam specialists like Joe Newport and Paul Burke got to work in Louisiana and Texas, the Alexandria headquarters buzzed with the knowledge that the center was living through one of the biggest moments in its history.

"It was fast-paced and hectic, to say the least," said Larry Upchurch, the Team Adam coordinator and deputy director of the center's missing-children division. In Upchurch's days as an FBI agent, the activity inside the National Center that Friday would have been described as a "special" – an event so big that every agent is called onto the case.

The National Center had weathered major events, to be sure. Whenever a television show broadcasts the center's hotline during a high-profile case, workers field a torrent of calls. Still, no single event had ever called for mobilizing the group's massive resources. Until that week, that is, when the Department of Justice asked the center to set up a special Katrina hotline.

In the space of three days, the center activated Project Alert, the group's nationwide corps of retired law enforcement officers. Airline tickets needed to be arranged and hotel rooms located for the 120 Project Alert volunteers who would be staffing the hotline. Sun Microsystems expanded the bandwidth of the website, which during the height of the post-Katrina evacuation would get 20 million hits a day.

In a first-floor room normally reserved for training, logistics specialists set up a brand-new call center. "It looked just like Jerry Lewis," Upchurch said.

Project Alert volunteers worked 12-hour shifts at long rows of tables, armed with only a telephone, a pad of paper and a pen. When calls came in, volunteers took down the information on paper forms. Eventually, the cases would be analyzed using a giant Katrina-only database that was under construction. But in those early days – before the special Katrina-only hotline went live on Monday, September 5 – a copy of each missing-kids case went not only to data-entry workers, but also upstairs to the second floor, where a dozen case managers and their assistants were furiously trying to keep up with demand.

Stacie Dotson, an assistant case manager, sat at her computer and set to work. In many of the cases, she and her colleagues had little to go on. In one memorable example, a mother called to say she had left her eight-month-old baby in the care of a sitter named Yolanda – no last name. Other times, spellings were inconsistent or else important details were forgotten in the trauma of the evacuation.

Dodson and the others started by compiling a list of every known shelter – the number was growing by the hour – and asking workers there if they knew anything. They checked web postings and made cold calls to hotels, churches and even prisons.

"We weren't throwing our hands up in the air," said Charles Picket, a senior case manager. "We tried to say, 'All right, let's look at the sites. Did anybody make a report for a child with this description?'"

As she worked at her desk, Dodson sifted through the handful of faxes from Joe Newport in Baton Rouge.

Despite Newport's efforts, Dodson had little to examine. Few of the children even had names or exact ages. There was a 6-year-old whose name had been spelled Deamonte Love on the fax. He had a little brother with the unusual name of Darynael Williams. And there was a two-year-old girl with thick braids and wide eyes. "Possibly named Gabby," the fax read.

Then she flipped through a stack of reports sent from Paul Burke in San Antonio. Even though it was only Saturday, Burke had already sent over several reports of parents who had lost their children.

Dodson's eye suddenly stopped. Here was a mother named Marceline Alexander. She was missing a two-year-old girl named Gabrielle.

Gabrielle. Gabby. Could it possibly be?

It was worth a shot.

Dodson dialed Newport.

"We have a possible match," she said.

Reading from the list of shelter contacts, Dodson recited to Newport the number of Tim Gebel, the Child Protective Services administrator who was running the missing-persons operation at KellyUSA in San Antonio.

Gabel gave him the number of Ada Gomez, a CPS supervisor who was on duty.

Gomez had been busy all day since reporting for her shift at 11 a.m. that morning.

Now that the evacuees had showered, eaten and had a night's sleep, reunification became their next priority. All day Saturday, they flooded Room 311. Sometimes guards brought in children who had become separated from their parents within the shelter. There was often nothing the CPS workers could do but watch the kids and wait for the parents to show up.

Then Gomez's cell phone rang. She glanced at the screen.

That's odd, she thought. Her caller ID flashed "Virginia" and a 703 area code.

She didn't know anyone in Virginia. Busy as she was, Gomez considered letting the voicemail pick up. "Should I even answer this?" she thought.

"Hello?" she said.

Joe Newport was on the other line.

He was in Baton Rouge. They had seven kids who had lost their parents, Newport explained.

"Can you see if anyone has listed them missing?" Newport asked Gomez. "I have a feeling their moms might be at Kelly."

"Sure. Let me get the notebook," Gomez answered.

Newport knew the name of the girl – Gabby, possibly Gabrielle – and had a description of what she was wearing. He also had a potential name for the mother: Marceline Alexander.

As Gomez flipped through the notebook, she couldn't help but wonder if the attempt was futile. In the 24 hours since evacuees began arriving at the shelter, the notebook had grown thick with intake forms. What are the odds, she thought.

Then Gomez's heart stopped. There it was. Marceline Alexander. Daughter named Gabrielle.

"Oh my gosh. There's no way," Gomez said. "You're not going to believe this. We have a match."

Chapter Fifteen
TEARS ON THE TARMAC

On the other end of the line, Newport remained calm.

"What are the odds that we could make this hit so quickly?" Newport remembers thinking. "My belief was that this Gabby was Gabrielle, but when you're talking about literally thousands of people, it was just a shot in the dark."

How did the mother describe the child, Newport asked.

Gomez scanned the intake form.

Gabrielle, according to Marcie, had been wearing a white shirt with green and blue flowers. She had on a pair of blue shorts that from the front looked like a skirt. On the morning of their rescue, Marcie had braided Gabrielle's hair into seven braids. Gabrielle was red-skinned, with a gap between her front teeth, Marcie had said.

The details matched.

"Can you find this mom?" Newport asked Gomez. "If you can find her, we're pretty sure you're going to find the other mothers, because all these kids are together. She's our missing link."

Gomez said she would try, and hung up the phone. But finding an evacuee on Saturday afternoon at KellyUSA was easier said than done.

By then, Building 171 housed close to 2,500 people and the numbers were growing by the hour. There was no public address system. Volunteers would eventually get bullhorns, but that was days away.

Posting a sign was also out of the question. By Saturday, nearly every available space along the walls had been covered in messages and notes. Another sign would just get lost in the sea of paper.

So Gomez ripped out a piece of notebook paper and uncorked a red marker. "MARCELINE ALEXANDER," she wrote. Then she and a coworker wandered the halls, calling her name and carrying the sign.

Ten minutes passed, then 20. Still no luck. Finally, about 45 minutes after they set out, a man walked up to Gomez and her colleague.

"Why are you looking for her?" he asked. "I know that person."

"We think we found her children. It's very important that she come see us."

"I'm pretty sure I can find her," he said.

"Tell her to come back right away. Room 311."

Marcie and Yowanda were sitting on their cots when they saw Leewood, Yowanda's boyfriend, come jogging toward them.

"Marcie," he said. "They found Gabby."

Within minutes, Marcie was on the line with Joe Newport.

Once again, Newport was hesitant to jump to conclusions. Describe your daughter to me, he asked her.

"She's red-skinned," Marcie said. "She's got big eyes, and she's two years old."

She ran through the details about the shirt, the shorts, the braids. That did it.

"That's her," Newport told Marcie. "We have her."

Marcie looked over at Yowanda. "Oh my God," she said. "I can't believe this."

Then Yowanda described Leewood, Jr. Sure enough, the picture matched the little boy all the Big Buddy workers were calling G.

Newport ran De'Monté's name by Yowanda and Marcie. It sounded familiar.

"Get the other mothers," he said. "And call me right back."

Newport's certainty grew with each mother he spoke to.

"I think we have your kids," Newport told Catrina.

"Oh my God, are you serious?" Catrina said. "Thank you, thank you, thank you!"

Newport explained that Big Buddy workers were caring for the children. They were having a lot of fun, he said. Would you like to talk to De'Monté? Newport asked.

Would she ever.

"Hey sweetie," Catrina crooned into the phone.

"Hey, Mama," De'Monté answered, tight-lipped as ever.

"I miss you," she said.

"I miss you too."

"What you doing?"

"Nothing."

"You watching after your brother?"

"Yeah."

"Are the other kids being good?"

"No," De'Monté said. "Some of them are being bad."

Newport got back on the phone. "I want you to do me a favor. Tell the other mothers not to leave."

In San Antonio, Paul Burke listened as the mothers celebrated. But he hesitated about joining in.

"There was always a chance that maybe we didn't have the kids that we thought we had," Burke said. "I know the parents were a lot more excited than we were."

Now that Burke and Newport were fairly sure they had matched the right kids with the right mothers, the next task was to reunite them. The most likely answer would be to either fly the mothers to Baton Rouge, or fly the kids to San Antonio.

Getting a plane wouldn't be a problem. Angel Flight, a volunteer program in which pilots fly their own planes on humanitarian missions, had been at work in Louisiana almost since Hurricane Katrina hit the state. Through an arrangement with the federal Department of Homeland

Security, Angel Flight pilots are tasked with helping out during national emergencies, working not as first responders but rather as backup support. With their small private planes, Angel Flight pilots can get people in and out of places that bigger planes cannot. Now, in the aftermath of the hurricane, Angel Flight pilots were ferrying medical patients and stranded children to destinations all over the country.

If the mothers went to Baton Rouge, they would join the hordes of evacuees that had already overwhelmed the city, taxing its services to the point where gas and food were starting to run out. San Antonio, on the other hand, was pulling out all the stops for the evacuees. They'd be able to find apartments and get jobs without competing with tens of thousands of other New Orleans residents.

Another factor in favor of sending the children to San Antonio was the kids' size. It would take only two small planes to fly seven children to Texas. "These kids are collectively only 200 pounds," Burke said. "It was more economical."

* * *

By Saturday night – around the time that Burke and Newport were arranging to reunite the families – word had spread within the LSU field house that the seven children had found their parents.

"I think every media station in the United States got my cell phone number," said Michael Keller. As the scene commander, he handled all the press inquiries. "I did more media interviews than I can count."

So many people were curious about the children that the security guard posted at the foot of the steps to the shelter had to limit access to Department of Social Services and Big Buddy workers alone.

After two days of serving as the children's spokesman, De'Monté decided that he was tired of cameras and reporters. "They would have all types of people coming in, trying to talk to him and get pictures of him," Derrick said. "He just decided he was tired of cameras."

Although the Big Buddy workers were relieved that the children would be reunited with their parents, they were disappointed that the mothers wouldn't be coming to Baton Rouge.

"We were like, please bring them to us. Please," Derrick said.

"We love your children," Jodi longed to tell Felecia, whom she only knew as Zarione's mother. Instead, she had to settle for a letter. That night, she told Felecia how attached she had become to both Zarione and Ty're. "Anything I can provide for them, I'll try to," she remembers writing. She copied down her cell phone number, and signed her name.

Ina, too, wrote a letter. In it, she listed the names and phone numbers of each Big Buddy worker, and who they had cared for. "I was like, call any number, whatever you need. Just call." Ina tucked the letter beside a photo of Derrick that she knew De'Monté treasured. That way she could be sure it wouldn't get lost.

The Big Buddy workers kept the kids busy that night, and tried not to think about the fact that they were spending their final evening together.

De'Monté, as energetic as ever, played on a treadmill at the end of the hall. "He would run!" Derrick said. "I was scared he was going to break his jaw because he liked to put it on as fast as it could go."

Someone brought in a basketball hoop, and Keller played ball with De'Monté and the older children who were also staying at the shelter.

The next morning, the Big Buddy workers prepared the children to meet their parents. Each kid got a bath and fresh clothes. "Their hair was freshly combed. We wanted their parents to see them at their absolute best," Kori said.

Terrell bought each child his own bag, and in it the workers stuffed everything they could imagine the mothers might need. Wet wipes. Diapers. Lotion. Shampoo. Conditioner. Barrettes and combs and brushes. "We just wanted to make sure that wherever they were, whenever they arrived, they had everything they could want," Kori said. "We didn't want their parents to have to want anything."

By Sunday morning, caring for the children had become the most natural thing in the world. If Da'Roneal wouldn't stop fussing, Ina would tell the others, "Just hand him to me."

"He just stopped crying," Jodi said. "He was fine."

It was early afternoon when it was finally time to leave the shelter. Each Big Buddy worker carried out the child he or she had grown attached to over the past three days. As they walked down the stairs, a crowd gathered.

"It was like slow motion," Lauren said.

Once outside, the workers strapped the children into car seats.

When Jodi lifted Zarione into the van, she looked back at her, confused. "Ok, let's go," Zarione said.

"No, you get in the van," Jodi said. Zarione gave her a hug.

"I love you," Jodi said.

"I love yooo-oo."

Jodi strapped Zarione into her car seat and shut the door.

"I was on the outside of the van and I was fine." Then Zarione began to cry. "Whoosh," Jodi said. "It was over."

Gabby cried, too. Ty're banged his fat little fist against the window.

Dejahney, whose face had been a rigid mask for days, broke into a huge grin.

"She was beaming," Jodi said. "It was like, Bye! See ya!"

"She knew she was going to see Mom," Ursula said.

De'Monté refused to get in the van.

"Do you understand?" Derrick asked him. "This is the big moment. You're gonna meet Mom."

"No," De'Monté said.

Derrick couldn't blame him. In the course of a week, this six-year-old had learned that nothing in life was certain. Why should he trust a promise that he was about to see his mom? Derrick decided to ride in the van as far as the airport. Brent Broussard, who had been caring for Dejahney, got in, too.

The van drove away, and the rest of the Big Buddy workers wrapped their arms into a group hug and cried.

*   *   *

Nearly 450 miles to the southwest, the mothers made their own preparations.

The Salvation Army had set up a "Distribution Center," a cavernous room inside Building 171 that workers were quickly filling with new and used clothes, toiletries, toys, diapers, and books.

Felecia and Catrina stocked up on clothes for the children, diapers, and toys. There were also lines for getting food stamps and other services, but they decided to wait on that. "We were just walking around, trying to get familiar with the place," Felecia said.

With the plane arranged through Angel Flight, Paul Burke realized he needed some way of getting the mothers to the airport. The bus needed to be big enough to carry him and the CPS workers, not to mention the children on the way back. Burke knew who to ask – Sherri Montez.

"I need a bus in 15 minutes," Montez remembers Burke telling her. At the time, Montez said, Burke thought the children had already left Louisiana. Burke told Montez he had to get the mothers to a private hangar at the San Antonio International Airport – quickly.

The deadline barely fazed Montez. She called Jerry Keifer, one of the bus drivers who was donating his time and services. Keifer was on his way to the hospital to drop off a family who was visiting a sick relative.

"Come back," she said. "We have to get this done."

131

Keifer dropped the family at the hospital, then turned his bus around. Montez dispatched another volunteer driver to the hospital to wait for those Keifer had left behind.

It was 5 p.m. by the time the mothers climbed onto the bus for the 16-mile ride to the airport.

Montez was expecting a celebration, but instead the mood was more of nervous anticipation. "They were not as excited as I thought," Montez said.

"They were very anxious to see their children again," said Jose Chapa, a Texas CPS worker. "It was pretty quiet."

When the bus pulled into Raytheon, a private terminal, the mothers discovered they were not alone. Word had spread about the pending reunion, and a throng of media trucks, cameramen and reporters were waiting when the bus arrived.

Felecia shied from the bright camera lights and microphones. "I thank God for you helping me find my children, but I don't want to be on camera," she told them.

Catrina, her father Adrian, Marcie and some of the others took their turns in front of the camera as they waited for their children to arrive.

Every plane that landed got a cheer from the women. "We were like, 'that's it, that's it,'" Keyshawn said. But the planes were always too big. The kids are on a small plane, the women were told. The pilots will call ahead on the radio.

A half-hour passed, then an hour. The late-summer sun slipped below the horizon. The mothers peered into the night sky, searching for the plane that would bring their children back to them. Whenever they asked what the holdup was, CPS workers told them to be patient. "You've got to wait," they said.

*   *   *

The drive to the airport in Lafayette, Louisiana, took about 45 minutes. When Derrick, Brent and the children arrived, yet another media crew greeted them. Someone had set up a few tables of food, and the children feasted on pickles and other snacks.

Derrick and De'Monté played one last game of hide-and-seek.

Meanwhile, Angel Flight pilots Barry Brazil and Tim Bryant prepared their planes. Despite the children's small size, fitting everyone in the small, six-seat planes – Bryant had a Piper Malibu Mirage, and Brazil a Beechcraft Bonanza – wasn't simple. Two social workers would make the trip in addition to the kids, and each child came with a bundle of belongings. "I was shocked at the volume of stuff," Bryant said.

After scavenging up enough car seats – Brazil remembered convincing a few airport workers to donate their own kids' seats – the planes were finally ready.

Brent and Derrick hugged everyone goodbye. They placed Gabby, Zarione, Ty're, and Dejahney on one plane, and the rest of the children on another. "They were all a little bit scared," Brent said.

Again, De'Monté refused to get on without Derrick.

"You're going to meet your mom," Derrick said.

"No," De'Monté answered. "I'm not leaving you. I want you to come with me."

Derrick had already asked Brazil and Bryant if he might be able to fly to San Antonio, but the small size of the planes prevented any last-minute passengers.

Bryant coaxed De'Monté onto the plane. "You're going to be my co-pilot," he said.

De'Monté was resolute. "No," he said, tightening his grip on Derrick, who held him on his hip. "I need you to come with me."

Bryant and Brazil had hoped to make the flight in daylight, but as the minutes ticked by, both realized that was becoming increasingly impossible. They needed to leave.

There was no other choice. Derrick untangled the boy's arms from around his neck and set him down.

"He just gave up and pushed my head away," Derrick said. De'Monté sulked as he climbed onto the plane and into the co-pilot's seat.

Derrick felt sick. He had just broken the heart of a six-year-old boy.

The planes taxied along the runway and took off.

Derrick let the tears roll down his face. As the planes disappeared in the sky, Derrick said goodbye one more time. "Well, De'Monté, you're on your own," he said.

*　　*　　*

Aboard his Piper Malibu, Bryant eyed De'Monté nervously. Because of the plane's small size, Bryant had had no choice but to put the boy next to him in the co-pilot's seat.

But from previous experience flying with children, Bryant knew to be wary of curious boys. His plane was outfitted with dual controls, meaning all of the switches, gauges and buttons that Bryant used to fly the plane had doubles on the co-pilot's side of the plane.

One time, while flying a sick boy from Houston to Alabama, Bryant promised the child that when they reached cruising altitude, he would let him fly the plane for a little while. But to Bryant's surprise, the boy grabbed the throttle and pulled hard during takeoff. The next thing Bryant knew, the plane's nose was pointing straight at the sky. Although Bryant managed to recover control, the experience made him wary of letting children sit in the co-pilot's seat.

Communication was difficult, not only because of the sound of the plane, but because De'Monté's New Orleans patois and Bryant's Houston drawl proved to be mutually incomprehensible. What's more, all three children cried in the back, keeping the social worker busy.

To ease both of their nerves, Bryant tried to occupy the boy, who fidgeted and tried to unbuckle the seatbelt. "Draw me a horse," Bryant told De'Monté, pointing to the paper and pen that sat on the boy's lap.

"I can't draw that!"

"How about sports?" Bryant said. Soon, De'Monté was busy drawing basketball hoops, footballs and baseball diamonds.

The mood aboard Brazil's Beechcraft Bonanza was much more peaceful. Like kids on a long car trip, the children dropped off to sleep as soon as the plane was airborne. The Beechcraft cruised through clear skies.

Two hours after leaving Lafayette, Brazil began his descent toward San Antonio. Just to make sure all of the kids were okay, he asked the social worker to wake them up before landing.

But instead of crying over the interruption of their nap, the children sensed something good was about to happen. "They were happy," Brazil said. "It's like they knew that they were going to meet their parents. There was a sense of calm about the kids that they didn't have when they got on the plane."

*   *   *

It was 8 p.m. by the time the first plane arrived in the sky.

As soon as security opened the doors, the women ran in unison toward Bryant's Piper Malibu. But when the pilot opened the doors, only Catrina and Yowanda screamed with joy.

There sat De'Monté, Da'Roneal, and Leewood.

Leewood yelled "Mommy!" and Yowanda ran toward him. "I couldn't do nothing but cry," she said. "Because I thought I was never going to see him again."

Catrina, on the other hand, didn't shed a tear. "We had enough of tears," she said. "All I wanted to do was hold my kids."

135

She tried to ignore the cameras that were now recording her every move, but it was hard. "When they opened up the doors, the cameras just straight lit up," she said. "You couldn't even grab your kids."

Less than ten minutes later, Brazil's Beechcraft touched down.

Zarione was crying. She had soiled herself on the plane. Ty're laughed when he saw his mom, and screamed his nickname for her. "Fefe! Fefe!' he called.

Dejahney couldn't get out the plane fast enough. "She saw me and she started crying, trying to get out of the car seat," Keyshawn said. She was startled to see Dejahney in different clothes. In the excitement of reunification, she didn't realize that the clothes her daughter had been wearing were likely filthy. "I just grabbed her and we both started crying together," Keyshawn said. "She was holding me tight."

As the mothers held their children, Paul Burke breathed a sigh of relief. In the back of his mind, he had worried about making a huge mistake. Would the wrong children get off the plane?

But one look at the scene on the tarmac and he knew he had succeeded.

"We were sure when they saw their mamas," he said. "That was the telltale sign."

Chapter Sixteen
A NEW START

Major Steven Trisler couldn't sleep.

In the days after he said goodbye to De'Monté on Interstate 10, he couldn't shake the images of those seven children. Had he made the right decision to separate them from their neighbor, Shawn Jackson? Had he set them adrift in the horror of post-hurricane New Orleans?

Since leaving the children, Trisler had seen a lot of things. There was the chaos of the Superdome, where he again helped load evacuees onto buses. There was the convention center, where children stepped around dead bodies and families pushed sick relatives in shopping carts.

There was the boy's football helmet that Trisler had found in the debris of Interstate 10 and Causeway Boulevard. Where was that boy now? Trisler wondered. Had he grabbed the helmet as he escaped the flood, hoping he'd still be able to go to football practice?

There were plenty of other images that stuck with Trisler. But he couldn't stop thinking about those seven kids. The little girl with braids in her hair, who had screamed her little head off as he carried her away from Shawn Jackson. That baby and his big, round eyes.

Trisler had memorized the basic details of the children's story, so that if it came up later, he would remember which kids they were. The oldest was De'Monté Love. He had two cousins. They lived on the 3200 block of Third Street in New Orleans.

Finally, several days after saying goodbye to the children, Trisler was working at the airport when he ran into a high-level Department of Social Services worker.

"I had a bunch of kids down at the Causeway," Trisler told him. "Have we got that solved yet?"

"Was it seven kids?" the worker asked.

Trisler nodded. "One's name was De'Monté?"

"Yeah," the worker said.

"A four month old baby?" he asked.

"Yeah, we got them in Baton Rouge," the worker said. "Oh, and we found their parents. Their parents were in San Antonio."

Trisler breathed out. All of the anger that he had been living with – anger that seven kids could have gotten separated from their parents, anger that their parents hadn't shown up on I-10, anger that Trisler was the one who had to deal with it – melted away as the DSS worker spoke.

"I knew then that I had closure on that issue," he said.

*   *   *

Like Trisler, the Houston ambulance workers couldn't stop thinking about those children.

"I wondered if they were all right, where they went," said Raymond Massie. "If they were just thrown off in the system and shuffled around."

After leaving the kids in the hands of Department of Health workers, Massie and the other ambulance workers had returned to I-10, making countless runs between New Orleans and Baton Rouge. "But kids always stay with you," Massie said.

One day, several days later, Massie passed a woman from the Department of Social Services. He asked about the children.

"Oh! We meant to tell you," she said. "They found the families for all of them."

Massie whooped. "YEAH!" he shouted, so loud that others in the hallway turned around to stare. "It really made my day."

Once back in the ambulance, Massie delivered the news to Coveney and Sizemore.

"It was just amazing," said Sizemore. "I'll never forget that day. I mean, as long as I live."

* * *

Back in Baton Rouge, local television carried the reunion of the children on the evening news. Jodi McKenzie and the rest of the Big Buddy workers watched with a divided heart. Already, they felt the absence of the children who had once relied on them like moms and dads.

In the days that would follow, the Big Buddy workers leaned on each other for support. "That was all we talked about!" Derrick Robertson said.

"We just had to hug each other," Kori Thomas said.

Derrick memorized a card De'Monté presented to him on their last day. "To Derek," it reads. "I like how you give big hugs and lift me up. You are a good friend. De'Monté Carlos Love."

As Jodi watched the reunion between Felecia and Zarione, she peered at the television closely. Unable to give up the caregiver role entirely, she looked at the screen and wondered, "Does she have her bag?"

* * *

In the week after the reunification, mothers and children alike clung to each other.

"All she wanted me to do was to hold her. To not put her down," Marcie said.

Likewise, Marcie kept waking up in the middle of the night, just to check that Gabby was still sleeping beside her.

After days of being given anything her heart desired, Felecia noticed that Zarione was spoiled rotten. "Once she got back to me, she just felt she could do the same thing to me," Felecia said. "She just was happy with having her way. But she finally realized she was back with me."

Within two months of their ordeal, the five mothers of 3223 Third Street had scattered across Texas, and even to Georgia.

Yowanda moved to Atlanta with her boyfriend, Leewood Sr., and their son. Her brother has a house there, and they're staying with him. But Yowanda doesn't want to put down roots. Her mother is already making plans to return to New Orleans, and Yowanda plans to follow soon afterward. Another brother visited her old apartment and discovered that nearly all of her belongings were lost to mold and dampness – during the storm, rainwater had leaked into the apartment.

"There was nothing I could do," Yowanda said. "It's just something I lost. I can try to gain it back."

Marcie, too, left San Antonio soon after reuniting with Gabby. Her sister, a registered nurse, had fled before the storm to Dallas, and she invited Marcie to join her there.

Garland, the Dallas suburb where Marcie and Gabby now live, is a far cry from the Central City neighborhood that Marcy grew up in. With a median yearly income of $49,000 a year, the city's 217,000 residents are mostly middle and upper-middle class. About two-thirds of Marcie's new neighbors are white, with Hispanics making up a quarter of the population and blacks about 12 percent.

Marcie and Gabby live on a four-lane street in a neighborhood that is filled with apartment complexes like theirs – brick two-story buildings with tidy landscaping, pools and well-lighted parking lots. Without a car, Marcie is left to shop in the stores she can walk to, which include a Pizza Hut, a Taco Bell, and a Blockbuster video store.

The City of Garland, which took in about 2,200 hurricane evacuees, is paying Marcie's rent for the first three months. After that, she'll be on her own. The apartment is so nice she worries how she'll pay the $625 rent when her time runs out. She's started to look for jobs – service jobs, mostly, either in fast-food restaurants or at a store like Wal-Mart – but until the rent runs out, she says, she's in no rush.

She and Gabby share a two-bedroom apartment that comes with two full baths, a wood-burning fireplace, and a terrace. Through the city's Hurricane Relief Center – a one-stop shopping center for Garland's evacuees – Marcie has sparsely decorated her new living room with an oriental rug, a magazine rack, a fire screen, a brass coat rack, and a large mirror for mantle. She's filled her bedroom with a second-hand dresser, a television, a stereo, and a bed that was a hand-me-down from a cousin.

"I liked it the first moment I walked in here," Marcie said. "It looked like it was a quiet neighborhood."

Her apartment is easily the nicest she's ever lived in, and yet sometimes it feels like a gilded cage. Many nights, she and Gabby sleep at her sister's apartment, which is a few miles away. With no job, Marcie spends many days on her bed with Gabby, watching daytime talk shows through the fuzzy reception.

"I'm so bored here," Marcie said. "I don't have anything to do."

Gabby, a resilient little two-year-old, seems unfazed by her weeklong adventure in hurricane-ravaged Louisiana. Pictures of helicopters make her eyes light up. When she sees one in the sky, she squeals with a delight and points skyward. "Helicoppa, mama," she says. "Helicoppa!"

Keyshawn hasn't been as lucky. Of all the children, little Dejahney seems to have taken the ordeal the hardest.

"Some days she has her good days, and other days it's just awful," said Patricia Carter, Keyshawn's mother. Dejahney's already legendary temper has gotten even worse. She throws tantrums that last for hours.

"She goes into a crying spell where you just can't stop her," Patricia said. "I don't care what you do, you just can't stop."

One night, someone pulled a fire alarm in the shelter and authorities forced everyone outside. While they waited, a helicopter hovered overhead.

"No, no, no, no!" Dejahney screamed. She held onto Keyshawn so tight, Patricia said, she nearly choked her.

At night, Dejahney sleeps so close to her mother than she nearly smothers herself. Dejahney's trauma has her grandmother and mother alike at their wits' end.

"To listen to somebody crying constantly for two or three hours nonstop, at some point or another I get to feeling like I'm at that breaking point," Patricia said. "So I walk off. That's the best thing for me to do."

A month after the reunification, Patricia, Keyshawn and Dejahney were still living at KellyUSA, sleeping on cots and waiting to be assigned an apartment in San Antonio. Patricia Carter didn't know how much longer she could wait.

"Sooner or later I'm gonna break down," Patricia said. "I've been trying to be really strong for everybody, but it's gonna come out. When I get my house, I know it's gonna come out…I feel it coming up, trying to get out of me, and I'm trying to just keep it under control."

Two weeks later, their cell phone was disconnected. They haven't been heard from since.

More than any of the other mothers, Felecia and Catrina have found themselves buffeted by the winds of fame. In the week after the reunification, the story of De'Monté Love and his heroic deeds flickered across the nation's television and computer screens, and his name appeared in the pages of most major newspapers.

Because Felecia and De'Monté share a last name, Felecia got much of the mail, which in addition to letters of good wishes also included clothes, toys, and cash.

One day at KellyUSA, about a month after the storm, Felecia collected her mail, only to find yet another package from a well-wisher. Standing outside the makeshift post office, she and Catrina eagerly opened the box. Discovering it contained clothes – De'Monté and all the children now had more than they could possibly wear – Catrina hoisted the box on her shoulder and walked toward the main building. "I'm gonna take this to the distribution center" she said. "But I'll search through for the name-brand stuff first."

Catrina has become the de facto spokeswoman for De'Monté and Felecia, who doesn't like the attention. Catrina has learned not to laugh when a television reporter asks her to read aloud a letter someone had sent as if she was reading it the first time – even though the fraud seems ridiculous. "Oh my god! I told this story so many times," she said, ticking off the reporters she had spoken to. "NBC, ABC, the team from Three Wishes [a reality show]. Inside Edition."

The fame hasn't always made their lives easier. Weeks after the reunification, Catrina was contacted by someone who claimed to represent a "big celebrity" who had offered to pay for a year's rent in a San Antonio apartment. Catrina and her family waited for weeks in a FEMA-paid hotel room for the promise to come through. But one company turned her rental application down, even though the apartment would be paid for, and another later reneged on their promise. Catrina claims they backed out because apartment management discovered she was black.

With her time running out in the hotel room, Catrina decided to get her own place – celebrity or no celebrity.

The apartment she found is just down the road from Felecia's new place, in a part of San Antonio that is suburban, residential and a far cry from the old neighborhood in New Orleans. More than 90 percent of Catrina and Felecia's neighbors live above the poverty line. Three-quarters are white, 6 percent are black, and about 32 percent are of Hispanic descent.

The complex isn't as nice as the one the celebrity might have paid for, but it's comfortable. "It's very friendly," Catrina said. There are two pools, a children's playground, a fitness room and a computer room that has access to the Internet.

The apartment itself has two bedrooms, two bathrooms, a dishwasher, and wall-to-wall carpeting. "The apartment is real fine," she said.

In November, Darryl and Catrina renewed their vows at the Family Life church, where they've become regulars at Sunday service.

But now that they're settled, she is beginning to worry about what happens next. She's frustrated that while FEMA is paying for Felecia's apartment for a year, for some reason she's only being reimbursed for three months. Her money ran out just after Christmas. She's also mad that she and Darryl have to pay the electricity themselves. "We're struggling," she said.

Catrina gets frustrated at people who suggest she should be looking for a job. Her baby, Da'Roneal, is only six months old. And Darryl has been looking for something he can do part time. She's frustrated that his work experience, building furniture at a factory in New Orleans, doesn't seem to impress potential employers. The fact that they're from New Orleans might have once helped his cause, but now Catrina doubts it gives him an edge.

"The job ain't the issue," she said, her voice rising. "Before all of this, our life was situated. It's hard and they're still making us stress. The rent down here is high, plus the utilities, that's not giving us a break."

De'Monté is thriving in the first grade at his new school. A few weeks after he started, his new teacher, Rebecca Dynes, read an article about him in a magazine after another teacher made the connection. Dynes remembers reading the article in the supermarket checkout line, and not being able to stop the tears. "This little boy is in my class," she told the checkout clerk. "You may not think it's a big deal, but I do."

She asked Catrina if she could tell the class, and Catrina agreed.

Dynes read the article to the class before dismissal one day. As the children were filing out, one of the little boys walked up to another teacher. "I wish I could be a hero like De'Monté," he said.

Several times a week, De'Monté and Derrick speak on the phone.

Even months after the storm, De'Monté is still getting attention. He is in the running for a Trumpet Award, an honor awarded by CNN to outstanding African-Americans.

Only a year earlier, the family was reeling from the death of a toddler, and trying to make a new start. Now, Catrina and Felecia find themselves in a similar situation – rebuilding a life from scratch. A year earlier, De'Monté struggled with the knowledge that he set a fire that led to his cousin's death. Even though he was only five, the two sisters know that he understands what happened.

Sometimes, when Felecia baby-sits him, she notices the boy looking at her. "Not staring at me," she said, "but I'll be talking to somebody and he just looks at me."

At times like that, Felecia longs to ask De'Monté what he's thinking. "Do you think I'm mad at you?" she imagines herself asking. Instead, she keeps quiet. Maybe someday, she says, she'll ask.

Catrina tries not to talk about the fire, and she's fiercely protective of her son, refusing to let others talk to him about it. "He really don't talk about it because he goes to crying," she said. Every once in a while, she said, they will touch on the subject. "I say so much, and there's so much I leave alone, because I don't want that to affect him. A lot of people say he's gonna deal with that when he gets older. You know, right now I just want him to be a child."

That goes for his fame, too. Sometimes she happily welcomes reporters into her home. Other times, she loses her temper, unsure of how all the attention will affect her son.

"My child is six years old," she said. "I want him to live normal."

TIMELINE

Tuesday, August 23:

—Meteorologists notice a knot of low pressure forming over the southeastern Bahamas. They label it Tropical Depression 12, or TD-12 for short.

Wednesday, August 24:

—Wind speeds increase and TD-12 is renamed Tropical Storm Katrina. It gathers strength and moves across the Bahamas toward Florida.

Thursday, August 25:

—With storm winds reaching speeds of 75 miles per hour, Katrina becomes a hurricane.

Friday, August 26:

—Hurricane Katrina moves across Florida, packing winds of 80 miles per hour, knocking out power to 1.3 million Florida customers and killing at least 11 people.

—Louisiana Governor Kathleen Babineaux Blanco declares a state of emergency.

Saturday, August 27:

—At 4 a.m., Katrina is 435 miles from the mouth of the Mississippi River. With top winds reaching 115 miles per hour, the storm is now a Category 3.

—At 10 a.m., the National Weather Service declares a hurricane watch for southeastern Louisiana.

—Later that day, President George W. Bush declares a federal emergency in Louisiana.

—In the afternoon, Governor Blanco and New Orleans Mayor Ray Nagin hold a joint press conference and urge those in the hurricane's path to evacuate.

—In the evening, Catrina calls Felecia at work and tells her to pack her things because their father is driving them out of town.

Sunday, August 28:

—At 1 a.m., storm trackers clock Katrina's wind speeds at 145 miles per hour, making the storm a Category 4.

—At 6 a.m., the winds have increased to 160 miles per hour. Katrina is now a Category 5. The National Weather Service warns the storm is "potentially catastrophic."

—At 9:30 a.m., Mayor Nagin issues a mandatory evacuation order. It is the city's first mandatory evacuation ever and the first emptying of an American city since the Civil War.

—Later that day, Catrina and Felecia decide not to evacuate after all. They plan to weather the storm at Catrina's house.

—That night, rain begins to fall in New Orleans.

Monday, August 29:

—At 6:10 a.m., Hurricane Katrina makes landfall in Plaquemines Parish. The winds have slowed slightly, to 125 miles per hour, making the storm a Category 3 when it finally hits land.

—At 10 a.m., Katrina makes landfall again, this time near the border between Louisiana and Mississippi. As it moves northeast over land, it gradually loses power.

—That morning, the storm surge sends water sloshing over the Industrial Canal, flooding parts of the city and neighboring St. Bernard Parish.

—Later that day, City Hall confirms reports that the crucial 17th Street canal had given way, sending water from Lake Pontchartrain into the city. Several parts of the city are now underwater.

—In the early evening, Felecia and others in Catrina's apartment building venture outside. The water has not yet arrived in their neighborhood. Several of the residents, including Felecia, walk to a nearby Winn-Dixie to get food and supplies.

Tuesday, August 30:

—That morning, floodwater arrives in Central City. The residents of Catrina's building watch as it slowly creeps up, inundating the first-floor apartments.

—With 80 percent of the city now underwater, emergency officials and the American public alike begin to grasp the enormity of the disaster.

—That afternoon, U.S. Army Major Steven Trisler gets orders to deploy to New Orleans from San Antonio with the Fifth Army.

Wednesday, August 31:

—Trisler leaves early that morning for the drive to Louisiana.

—As the situation in flooded neighborhoods gets increasingly desperate, evacuees descend in droves on rescue points and shelters, including not just the Superdome – the city's designated shelter of last resort – but also Lakefront Airport, the New Orleans convention center, and the intersection of Interstate 10 and Causeway Boulevard.

—Trisler arrives in Baton Rouge late that night, and gets orders to travel to Interstate 10 and help evacuate victims.

—Around the same time, Pat Coveney and his ambulance workers arrive at the Department of Health's emergency operations center in Baton Rouge. They are also sent to Interstate 10.

Thursday, September 1:

—That morning, Catrina and Felecia decide to leave their apartment, no matter what.

—Around noon, they flag down a helicopter. When the pilot explains they are only taking children, the sisters and three other mothers push their children onto the helicopter.

—A few minutes later, the children land at the intersection of Interstate 10 and Causeway Boulevard. Their caretaker, Shawn Jackson, enlists the help of Major Trisler, who notifies the Department of Social Services and asks for the children to be taken to Baton Rouge.

—In the late afternoon, Coveney and his men drive the children to Baton Rouge in an ambulance.

—Around the same time, a helicopter finally collects the women, and takes them to Lakefront Airport, in eastern New Orleans.

—Meanwhile, the children arrive at the Department of Health command center in Baton Rouge, where health care workers examine them.

—Later that night, they are collected by workers for Big Buddy, an after-school program in Baton Rouge. They take the children to a shelter at the Louisiana State University field house.

—That night, Michael Keller, of the National Center for Missing and Exploited Children, arrives in Baton Rouge. He sets up operations outside the children's shelter in the field house.

TIMELINE

Friday, September 2:

—After an uncomfortable night sleeping on boxes of water bottles, the women board a helicopter bound for the Louis Armstrong International Airport. There, they reunite with their father and other men from the apartment building. The group boards a plane for San Antonio.

—Joe Newport, of the National Center for Missing and Exploited Children, joins Keller in Baton Rouge. Keller assigns him the case of the seven children. Together, the two photograph each child and send what information they have to the center's headquarters in Alexandria, Virginia.

—The mothers arrive in San Antonio in the early afternoon. A nurse discovers Catrina has high blood pressure and she is rushed to the hospital. Meanwhile, the mothers meet with Texas Child Protective Services workers and Paul Burke of the National Center.

Saturday, September 3:

—Catrina is discharged from the hospital and returns to the shelter.

—Meanwhile, Stacy Dodson, an assistant case manager at the center's Alexandria headquarters, makes a connection between Marcie Alexander and her daughter, Gabby.

—After getting the news from Dodson, Newport calls Texas, where he speaks with Ada Gomez, a Texas CPS worker. She checks the records and confirms the match.

—Marcie speaks to Newport by telephone. The rest of the mothers also get on the phone, and Catrina speaks with De'Monté.

—After some debate, it is decided that the children will be flown to San Antonio the following day.

Sunday, September 4:

 —The Big Buddy workers get the children ready, then bid them a tearful goodbye outside the field house. Two workers accompany the children to the airport in nearby Lafayette.

 —The mothers board a bus bound for the San Antonio International Airport.

 —In Lafayette, Angel Flight pilots Tim Bryant and Barry Brazil board the children on the planes. They fly to San Antonio in clear weather.

 —The plane lands just after dusk, and the parents and children are finally reunited.

KATRINA BY THE NUMBERS

33,000: Number of calls fielded by hotline workers at the National Center for Missing and Exploited Children (NCMEC) in the days after Hurricane Katrina

4,956: Number of cases of children missing in Hurricane Katrina that were opened by the National Center for Missing and Exploited Children after the storm

442: Number of missing-children cases that remained outstanding as of Dec. 30, 2005

80: percent of New Orleans submerged by water in the days after Hurricane Katrina

284,000: Number of homes destroyed by Hurricane Katrina across the five affected states

1,300: Number of people killed by Hurricane Katrina across the five affected states as of Dec. 30, 2005

1 million: Estimated number of people displaced by the storm

Sources: NCMEC, Time Magazine, Associated Press

A NOTE ON SOURCES

On Thursday, September 1, *Newsday* photographer Robert Mecea and I were wandering among the crowd on Interstate 10 when a U.S. Army Major stopped and asked to borrow my notebook.

I hesitated for a moment – after all, I had a deadline to meet – but figured I couldn't say no to a man in combat boots and army fatigues. With nothing better to do until I got my notebook back, I listened in on the conversation he was having with a young woman who was sitting on the curb. On her lap fussed a baby boy. Around her were eight other children, most of them toddlers. Only two were hers, she told the man, who turned out to be Major Steven Trisler.

As I listened, the breadth of the disaster finally dawned on me. Here were seven children – including a four-month-old baby – whose parents may have sacrificed their own lives so that their children could live. I found Robert and told him to come quick. The photos he took appeared on the cover of *Newsday* the next day.

Aside from that moment on Interstate 10, the rest of the events I describe in this book were recreated based on interviews with those who lived through them. In late September, I traveled to Dallas and San Antonio to interview Marcie, Catrina, Felecia, and Keyshawn. About a month later, I returned to New Orleans, where I toured the mothers' neighborhood, Baton Rouge and other areas.

Actions, descriptive details, and dialogue in the book were compared with as many witnesses as I could find. Catrina and Felecia's father, Adrian Love, did not return several calls for comment. Paul Riley, the maintenance man who put the children in the helicopter, also did not return calls. After interviewing Shawn Jackson, the woman who cared for the children on Interstate 10, on the scene, I wasn't able to locate her again.

When details were not based on my own reporting, I have noted the sources below.

Chapter Two:

The details about Katrina's landfall, wind speed and the history of Louisiana hurricanes is from the website of the National Hurricane Center at www.nhc.noaa.gov/.

Emergency officials' fear of the "Big One" is from several sources, including the *Times-Picayune's* 2002 series "Washing Away," which ran between June 23 and June 27.

The estimate of the number of people displaced in Katrina varies widely, ranging from a quarter million to a million. Several sources cite the million figure, including the *Washington Post* and the *Christian Science Monitor*. About 225,000 people were left homeless by the San Francisco earthquake, according to the United States Geological Survey. Details about the earthquake can be found at http://quake.wr.usgs.gov/info/1906/casualties.html.

The poll of New Orleans residents about evacuating, conducted as part of a hurricane-preparedness drill, was described in several news articles, including one in *Newsweek* on Sept. 12, 2005 titled "The Lost City," by Evan Thomas. The number of Superdome evacuees was also cited in numerous articles, including the *Times-Picayune* on Sept. 12. The story, "Superdome laid waste by those who sheltered," was written by Jeff Duncan. The number in the convention center was from my own reporting in New Orleans, plus other sources, including the *Los Angeles Times* in an article, "'They Just Left Us Here to Die:' At the New Orleans

Convention Center, thousands waited days cut off from relief," written by David Zucchino.

Chapter Three:

The *Times-Picayune* stories that wrote about the fire were "Eastern N.O. blaze kills 2-year-old, injures infant; Smoke detectors may have averted tragedy, official says," May 28, 2004, by Tara Young; and "Boy hurt in blaze leaves hospital; his brother died of smoke inhalation," May 29, 2004 by Walter Gabriel, Jr.

Census data for Catrina and Felecia's neighborhood is based on my own analysis of data from the Census' American Factfinder website, which is at www.census.gov.

Hoffman elementary's poor performance comes from several *Times-Picayune* articles, including "School Shake-Up; Orleans Parish plan will shower money and personnel on students with the lowest scores and greatest needs," May 24, 2001, by Brian Thevenot. The school's closing is based on articles in the *Times-Picayune*, including "Five elementary schools to close; Middle schools might survive," June 1, 2005 by Brian Thevenot.

Chapter Four:

All descriptions of Katrina's approach, arrival, wind speeds, and other data were taken from the website of the National Hurricane Center, at www.nhc.noaa.gov/. The death toll in Florida and power outage information was also from the National Hurricane Center's website.

Governor Blanco's emergency declaration was taken from an archived press release on the state of Louisiana website at www.gov.state.la.us/.

Data about Hurricanes Betsy and Camille were also taken from the National Hurricane Center website.

President Bush's emergency declaration was taken from the White House press release archives, found at www.whitehouse.gov/news/releases/2005/08/.

Mayor Nagin's warning to New Orleans residents was taken from an Associated Press article posted Saturday, August 27, 2005 and titled "Louisianans Told: Head for Higher Ground." It was written by Mary Foster. His evacuation order came from several media sources. The Civil War reference is according to a September 12, 2005, *Newsweek* article titled "The Lost City," by Evan Thomas. CNN talk show host Keith Olbermann cited the same fact on his show, "Countdown," on August 30, 2005.

The paragraph about how many residents relied on public assistance comes from two *New York Times* articles. One ran on September 2 and was titled "Government Saw Flood Risk but not Levee Failure," by Scott Shane and Eric Lipton. Another ran on September 4, 2005, and was titled "A Delicate Balance is Undone in a Flash, and a Battered City Waits." It was written by Peter Applebome, Christopher Drew, Jere Longman, and Andrew C. Revkin.

Data about fictional Hurricane Pam was taken from several websites, including Louisiana State University, which participated in the drill, at www.lsu.edu/highlights/052/pam.html. The Federal Emergency Management Agency's news release about Hurricane Pam is at www.fema.gov/news/newsrelease.fema?id=13051.

A NOTE ON SOURCES

The *Times-Picayune* story about the DVDs ran on July 24, 2005, and was titled "In storm, N.O. wants no one left behind; Number of people without cars makes evacuation difficult." It was written by Bruce Nolan.

The headlines about the storm were taken from a Cox News Service story on Monday, August 29, 2005, written by Tony Plohetski; a Knight-Ridder News Service story (which ran in the *St. Paul Pioneer Press*), written by Erika Bolstad on Tuesday, August 30; and an unsigned editorial in the *St. Petersburg Times*, which also ran on Tuesday.

Details about the Industrial Canal and the 17th Street canal were taken from various media sources, including the *New York Times* article "A Delicate Balance is Undone in a Flash, and a Battered City Waits," which ran on September 4, 2005. It was written by Peter Applebome, Christopher Drew, Jere Longman, and Andrew C. Revkin.

Chapter Five:

Details about the mission of the Fifth Army can be found at their website, www.5tharmy.army.mil/FifthArmy/about/About.htm. Although the Fifth Army still participates in homeland security missions, much of that responsibility in recent years has been transferred to the Army's Northern Command, or NorthCom.

Chapter Seven:

Details about the decline of Jimmy Swaggart Ministries comes from a January 28, 1999, *Boston Globe* article titled "Humbler Times; Swaggart continues quest for cash, souls," written by Curtis Wilkie. Details were also taken from a December 28, 1998, *Seattle Times* article titled "Swaggart Still Preaches, but a lot fewer are listening," by Joe Mathews.

Chapter Eight:

Details about the Louis Armstrong Airport came from several news articles in addition to the women themselves. Some details were taken from a story in the *New York Times* titled "More troops and aid reach New Orleans; Bush Visits Area; Chaotic Exodus continues," which ran on Sept. 3 and was written by James Dao and N.R. Kleinfeld.

Other articles which described the scene include:

"Grim Triage for Ailing and Dying at a Makeshift Airport Hospital," *The New York Times*, Sept. 3, 2005. By Felicity Barringer and Donald G. McNeil Jr.

"'There was real heroism;' Workers rescue, tend to thousands," *The Washington Post*, Sept. 3, 2005. By Dafna Linzer and Peter Slevin.

"The airport becomes rescue central," *The Washington Post*, Sept. 1, 2005. By Peter Slevin.

Chapter Eleven:

Details about the Houston Astrodome were taken from an Associated Press story titled "The cavalry arrives: National Guard relief convoy rolls into New Orleans." It ran Sept. 3, 2005 and was written by Robert Tanner.

Chapter Twelve:

Details about the National Center's history and services were taken from interviews with National Center staff, as well as their website, www.missingkids.com. Financial data about the group was taken from its 2004 Annual Report.

A NOTE ON SOURCES

The study cited by the National Center was conducted by the State of Washington's Office of the Attorney General.

Chapter Fifteen:

The description of the National Center's headquarters is taken from several articles written when the center opened its new building, including "To Find a Missing Child; Family Realizes Goal of Seeing Center Dedicated," *The Washington Post*, by Patricia Davis, Sept. 16, 1999.

Descriptions of the National Center's activities and statistics come from its 2004 Annual Report.

The number of people at KellyUSA is according to a Sept. 3, 2005, article in the *San Antonio Express-News*, "Evacuees arrive in San Antonio," by Tracy Idell Hamilton.

Chapter Sixteen:

Details about Garland, Texas, were provided by the city's public information officer, Dorothy White. Census data about Catrina's new neighborhood was taken from the Census website.

ABOUT THE AUTHOR

Katie Thomas is a general-assignment reporter for Newsday. In 1999, she was named Best New Reporter by the New York Newswomen's Club, and has since worked on several award-winning projects, including two investigative series – one examining the influence of politics in the selection of Long Island judges, and another that uncovered cronyism and waste in Suffolk County's nationally-recognized land preservation program. In addition to the aftermath of Hurricane Katrina, Thomas has also covered major news events, including the terrorist attacks of 9/11, the crash of Flight 587 in Queens, and the blackout of 2003, for which Newsday was named a Pulitzer Prize finalist.